THE "REMEMBER WHEN" DOLLHOUSE

THE "REMEMBER WHEN" DOLLHOUSE

PHYLLIS GIFT JELLISON

VNR VAN NOSTRAND REINHOLD COMPANY
New York   Cincinnati   Toronto   London   Melbourne

Printed in the United States of America.
Designed by Loudan Enterprise

Published in 1978 by Van Nostrand Reinhold Company
A division of Litton Educational Publishing, Inc.
135 West 50th Street, New York, NY 10020, U.S.A.

Van Nostrand Reinhold Limited
1410 Birchmount Road
Scarborough, Ontario M1P 2E7, Canada

Van Nostrand Reinhold Australia Pty. Ltd.
17 Queen Street
Mitcham, Victoria 3132, Australia

Van Nostrand Reinhold Company Limited
Molly Millars Lane
Wokingham, Berkshire, England

16 15 14 13 12 11 10 9 8 7 6 5 4 3 2 1

Library of Congress Cataloging in Publication Data

Jellison, Phyllis Gift.
    The "remember when" dollhouse.

    Includes index.
    1. Doll-houses. 2. Doll furniture. I. Title.
TT175.3.J45   745.59'23   78-8127
ISBN 0-442-24128-3

Contents

Introduction

Not so long ago—say, fifty years or so—most Americans were born, raised, and lived out their lives in towns and small cities, where, according to Presidents Harding and Coolidge (themselves small-town boys), there was more real happiness per square mile than anywhere else in the world. In those days, before the Nation rushed pellmell into high-rise apartments and tract homes that hired writers called "chic" and "the ultimate in modern living," most people lived in houses that were built to stand up under the wear-and-tear of normal family life, and, equally as important, to look and actually *be* different from their neighbors'. These houses were designed by men without college degrees and were built by skilled craftsmen, who owned their own tools and took pride in the way they laid a floor or built a fireplace. The results were seldom classic. Terms such as Georgian and Victorian meant little to the men who constructed such houses and to the people who lived in them. They were built for utility and durability; almost as an afterthought, finely turned balustrades or fancy lattice skirts were added to the piazzas as a token concession to what then passed for beauty.

Millions of such houses were built in America between WWI and WWII. What seems most remarkable to us today is the fact that no two of them were the same—or so it seems in retrospect. Perhaps in reality, however, many of them originally were. They may have become distinctive only after use. There is no denying that after they had been lived in for a time, a strange thing happened: These simple, often awkward-looking, solid, and austere structures suc-cumbed to humanness and took on the character—one might even say the personality—of the families they housed. Some hardened and turned their nature inward behind a cheerless mask. Others mellowed and brightened, and to those of us who lived in or near them during those post-Armistice years, seemed the very essence of beauty and friendliness.

It is such a house, a happy house, that this book reproduces in miniature. It was built in 1919 and purchased for $5000. It was here that my husband was born and lived throughout his boyhood and it was here that his widowed mother, Glennie, kept house until her death last year. The old place, still standing and going strong, is now owned by strangers. To those of us who remember its earlier days, it will always be the house where my husband Charlie and his sister Pauline grew up, while Father Chic kept the fires going, and Glennie ruled the roost.

Insofar as possible I have furnished the house as it was during my husband's youth. To do this, I have relied upon my own memory of the pieces that were still in use when I first visited there in the early 1950s, upon snapshots from the family album, and upon the recollections of my husband and sister-in-law, Pauline Jellison Weatherbee, to both of whom I am most grateful for their help in the preparation of this book. I would also like to express my appreciation to my good friend, neighbor, and fellow-miniaturist, Mary Hinckley, for her innumerable helpful suggestions and unflagging moral support.

Let us now think in miniature.

The Dollhouse

TOOLS

Table saw (to cut the numbered pieces of the house)
Band saw (to cut shingles, clapboards, and trim)
Jig saw (to cut out the windows)
Drill, electric or hand drill
Yardstick
Calipers
T-square
Scissors
X-acto knife
Hammer
Screw driver
C-clamps
Mini-lathe (optional)

SUPPLIES

PLYWOOD
    2 sheets 5' × 5' × 1/4" for house
    3 sheets 4' × 4' × 1/16" for clapboards, trim, etc.
    1 sheet 42" × 30" × 3/4" for base

BASS WOOD
    1/4" square for balusters on porch
    3/8" square for posts
    4 lengths 3/8" × 1/8" for railings
    1 piece 36" × 3" × 1/8" for sills
    3 pieces 24" × 3" × 1/16" for plate rail and doors

Finishing nails, 1/2" and 1"
Screws, 3/8" × 4 (plain) flat-head wood screws
Glue
    Tite-bond for wood
    Soloman's Quik for acetate windows
    hot glue for wood partitions (optional)
Paint
    1 gal. white acrylic
    1 pt. black acrylic
    1 pt. dark green acrylic
    gray enamel for porch floor
Sandpaper
    4 sheets medium garnet
    2 pieces black, coarse, 3M Crystal Bay emery cloth for roof
Acetate 40" × 8" for "glass" windows and doors
Pin hinges, 2 sets for attic and bath openings (small)

Screw eyes and hooks, 2 sets, for closing front and back (optional)
Contact paper, 4 yards pine pattern for floors
Stain, 1 pt. dark mahogany and 1 pt. Puritan Pine Minwax
Wallpaper for 5 rooms and halls
Wallpaper paste
Brick dollhouse paper, 1/2 yard or 3 sheets for cellar base and chimney
Door knobs, 4 miniature sets, brass
Mylar paper, 1 piece frosted for front door
Plastic wood, small tube for filling nail holes (optional)
Lifelike grass (optional)
Decoupage Super Bond spray (optional)
Brushes
Pencils, carpenter's flat, lead pencil and grease pencil for marking acetate
Piano hinges, 2, each 17 1/2" long

DIRECTIONS
MAIN HOUSE

1. Draw the outside dimensions of the basic house (27 1/2" × 24" without shed or bay front) onto the base (Fig. 1). Rectangle will be 3" from sides of base, 7 1/2" from back, 7" from front. Mark accordingly. NOTE: All lumber for the construction of the house is cut from 1/4" stock (preferably plywood) unless indicated otherwise. Drilling holes for the nails will prevent the wood from splitting. Screws may also be used throughout the house construction at stress points. Nail or screw at least an inch from the ends. (Titebond glue takes at least a half hour to set.)

2. Cut two pieces 27 1/2" × 1 3/4" × 1/4" for the cellar sides. Cut three pieces 23 1/2" × 1 3/4" × 1/4" for the ends and middle support. Always cut with the grain when possible.

3. Glue and nail the cellar ends between the cellar sides and then glue and nail rectangle (27 1/2" × 24" wide × 1 3/4" high) onto the base. Glue and nail the middle support centered between the cellar sides.

4. Cut out five pieces (two each of A and C) for the first floor. Cut out pieces #1 through #17 (Fig. 3 through 10). Piece #17 is 2 1/2" × 11/16" × 1/4" and fits between the side pieces of the steps to form the door opening to the cellar. NUMBER ALL PIECES AS SOON AS CUT. Set aside first floor pieces (Fig. 2) and pieces #4, #14, #15, and #16 until later.

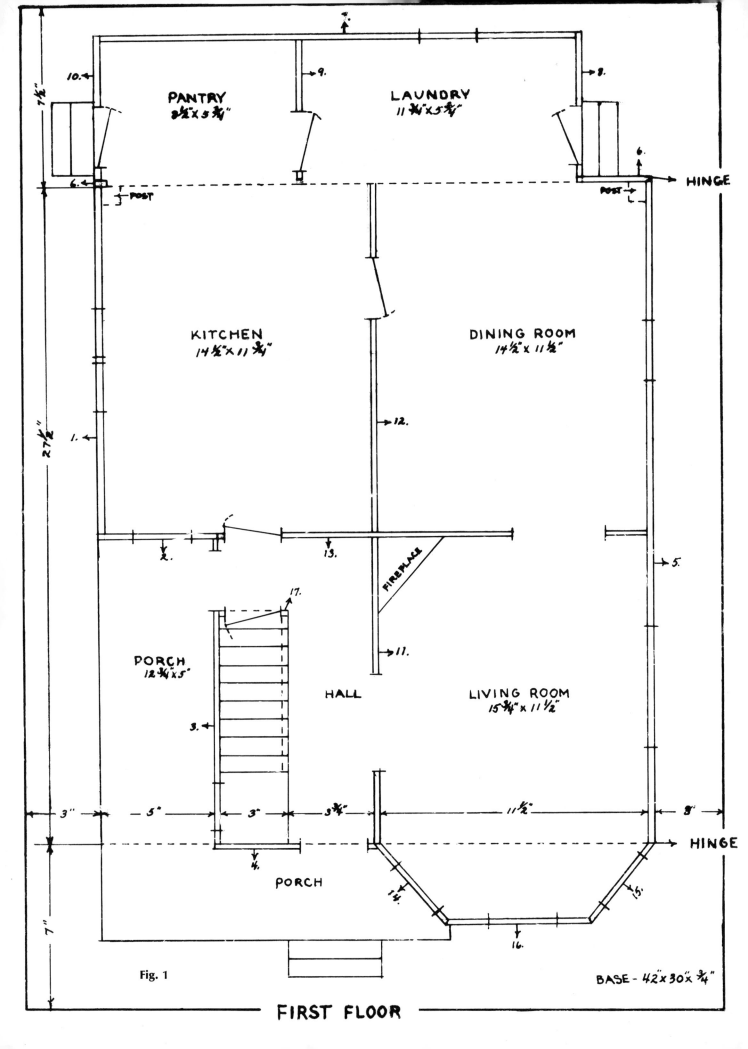

FIRST FLOOR

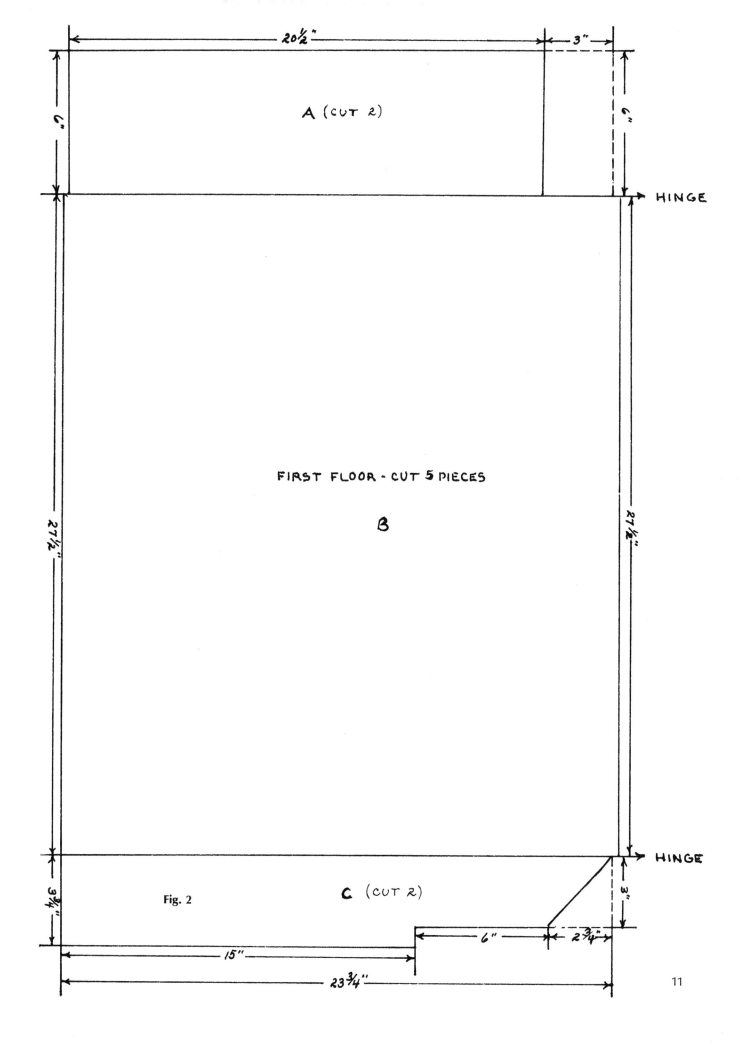

A (CUT 2)

20½"

3"

6"

6"

HINGE

27½"

27½"

FIRST FLOOR - CUT 5 PIECES

B

HINGE

3¾"

Fig. 2

C (CUT 2)

3"

6"

2¾"

15"

23¾"

11

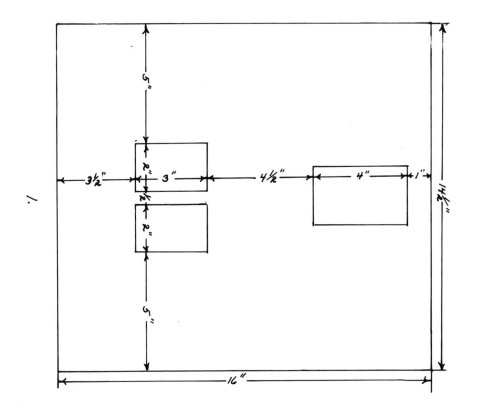

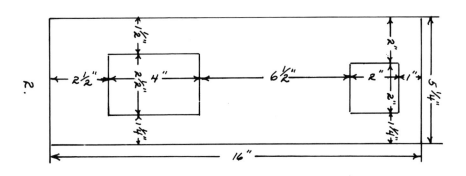

Fig. 3

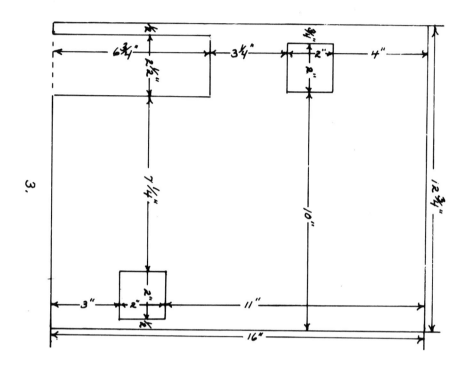

3.

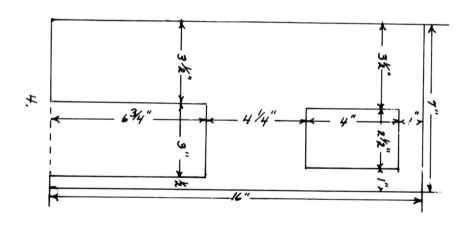

4.

Fig. 4

13

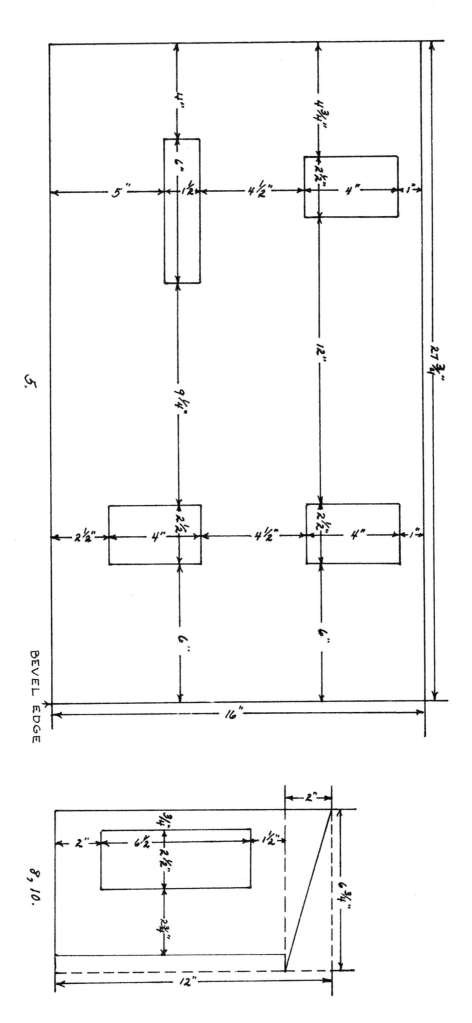

Fig. 5

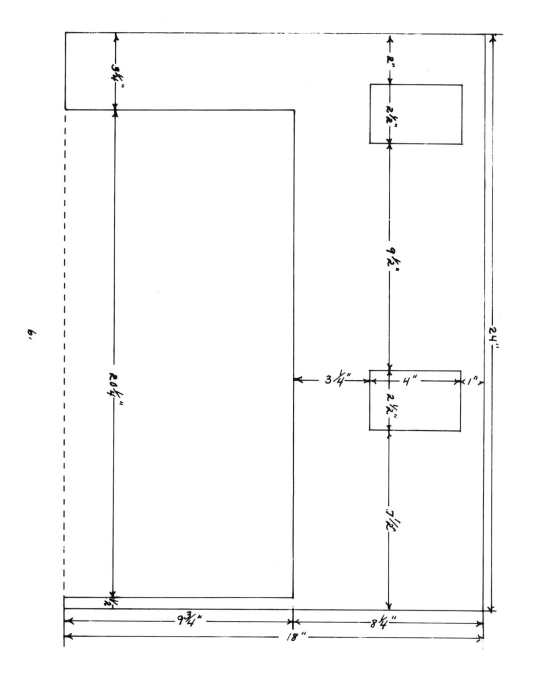

Fig. 6

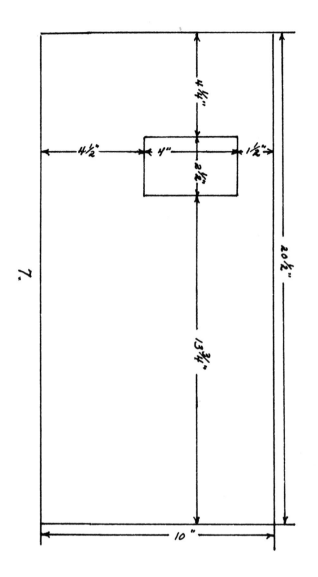

7.

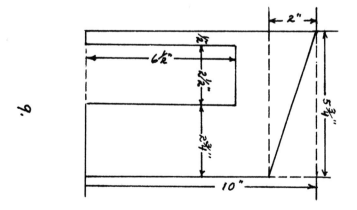

9.

Fig. 7

16

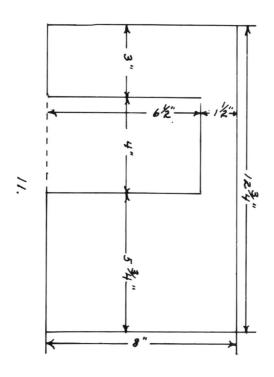

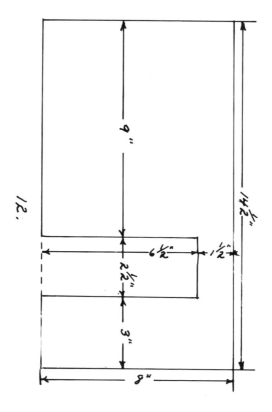

Fig. 8

17

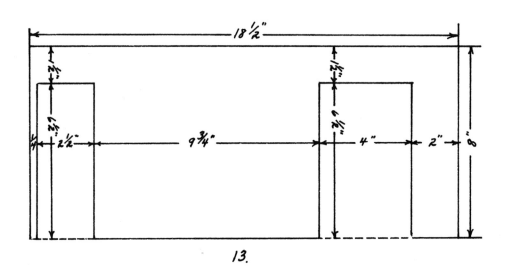

13.

Fig. 9

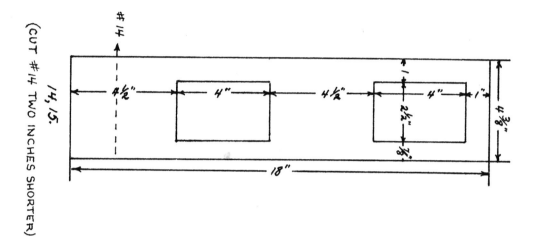

14, 15.

#14

(CUT #14 TWO INCHES SHORTER)

4½" 4" 4½" 4" 1"

1" 2½" ⅛" 3⅛"

18"

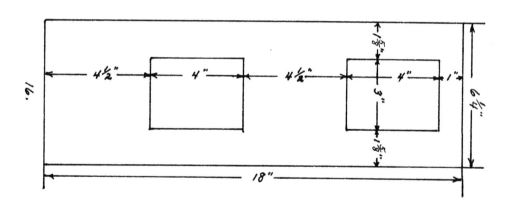

16.

4½" 4" 4½" 4" 1"

⅛" 3" ⅛" 6¼"

18"

Fig. 10

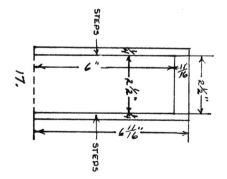

17.

STEPS

6" 15/16 2½"

2½"

6 11/16"

STEPS

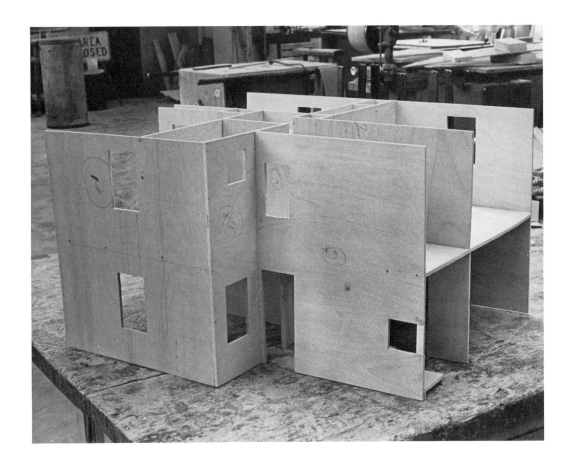

5. Glue and nail #1 and #2 at a right angle. Refer to Fig. 1 to see the connecting positions. Be sure the windows and doors are right side out. Do not nail to base.

6. Glue and nail #3 at a right angle to #2.

7. Glue and nail #13 to #5 and #2.

8. Glue and nail #11 and #12 to #13.

9. Cut out the two sides (6 3/4″ × 6 1/4″ × 1/4″) for the first floor steps (Fig. 11).

10. Cut two stair landings 3″ × 3″ × 1/4″ and two pieces 3″ × 1/2″ × 1/4″ for the base to support the lower landing.

11. Glue lower landing to base pieces and then to the wall #3.

12. Glue one side of steps to wall #3 and lower landing.

13. Glue and nail upper landing to wall #3 at top of steps, exactly 7/16″ above last step, as shown in Fig. 11.

14. Glue other side of steps to lower landing.

15. Glue #17 between the back side pieces of steps to form top of basement doorway (Fig. 10).

16. Cut two pieces (A and B) for the second floor. (Fig. 13). Set aside front bay floor piece until later. Glue and nail other second floor piece to tops of room partitions of first floor and against walls.

17. Cut out two step side pieces for the *first* floor upper landing. Landing detail is shown in Fig. 12. (Ignore the optional cutting line for the side covers until later in step 35.)

18. Glue upper landing step sides to the underside of the second floor and onto landing.

19. Cut stair risers and treads (Fig. 11) and glue to all steps, risers first, including upper landing. (I did this later, as seen in the photos, but subsequently discovered that it is difficult to reach the landing steps after the third floor is placed.) Stain and carpet the landing steps now, while they are still accessible.

20. Cut out pieces #18 through #30 (Fig. 14 through 17).

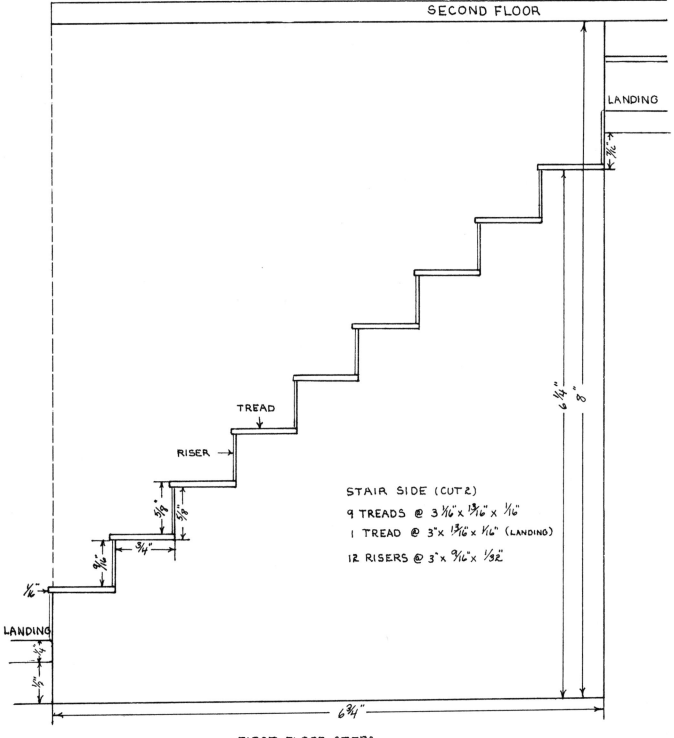

SECOND FLOOR

LANDING

$\frac{7}{16}$"

TREAD

RISER

$\frac{5}{8}$"

$\frac{5}{8}$"

STAIR SIDE (CUT 2)

9 TREADS @ 3$\frac{1}{16}$" x 1$\frac{3}{16}$" x $\frac{1}{16}$"

1 TREAD @ 3" x 1$\frac{3}{16}$" x $\frac{1}{16}$" (LANDING)

12 RISERS @ 3" x $\frac{9}{16}$" x $\frac{1}{32}$"

$\frac{9}{16}$"

$\frac{3}{4}$"

$\frac{1}{16}$"

6$\frac{1}{4}$"

8"

LANDING

$\frac{1}{4}$"

$\frac{1}{2}$"

6$\frac{3}{4}$"

FIRST FLOOR STEPS

Fig. 11

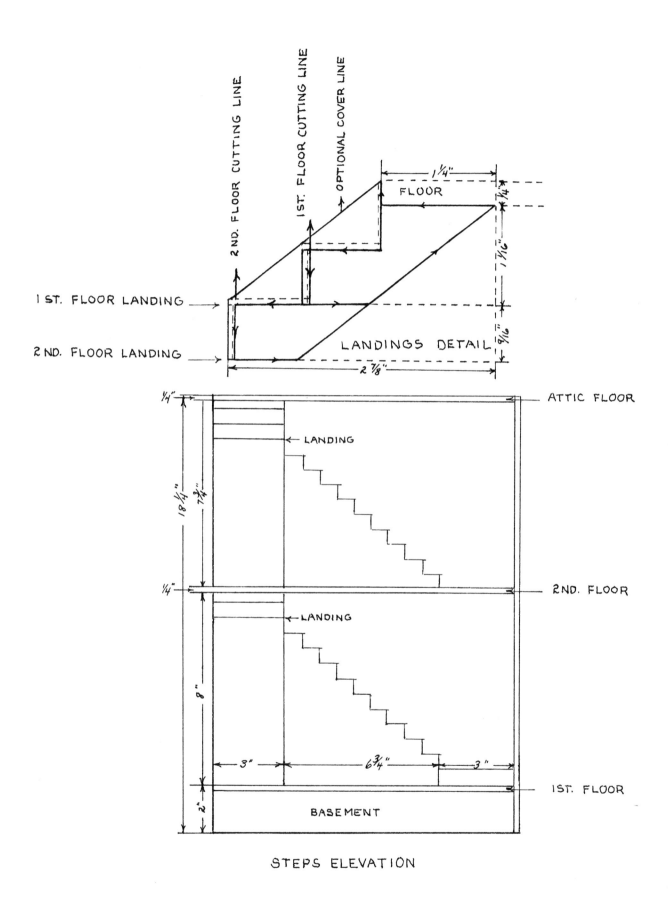

2ND. FLOOR CUTTING LINE

1ST. FLOOR CUTTING LINE

OPTIONAL COVER LINE

FLOOR

1¼"

¼"

1¹³⁄₁₆"

1ST. FLOOR LANDING

2ND. FLOOR LANDING

LANDINGS DETAIL

⁹⁄₁₆"

2 ⁷⁄₈"

ATTIC FLOOR

¼"

LANDING

18½"

7¾"

LANDING

¼"

2ND. FLOOR

8"

3"

6¾"

3"

1ST. FLOOR

2"

BASEMENT

STEPS ELEVATION

Fig. 12

23

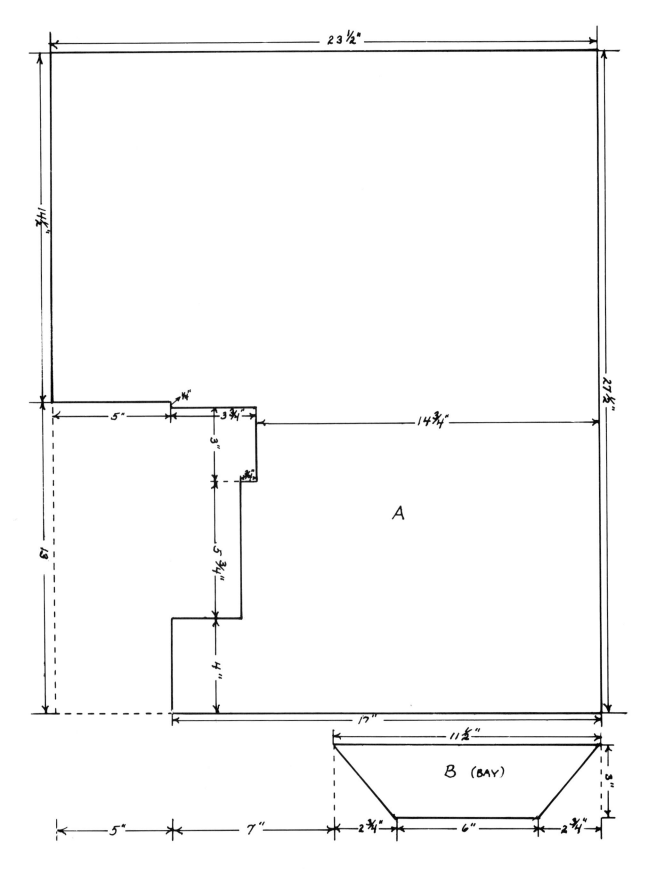

SECOND FLOOR (CUT 2 PIECES)

Fig. 13

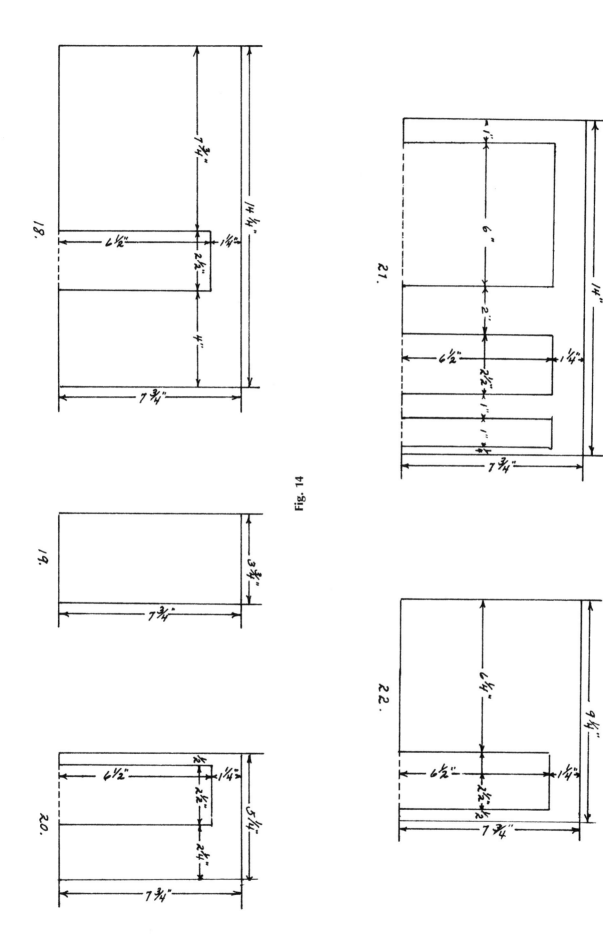

Fig. 14

Fig. 15

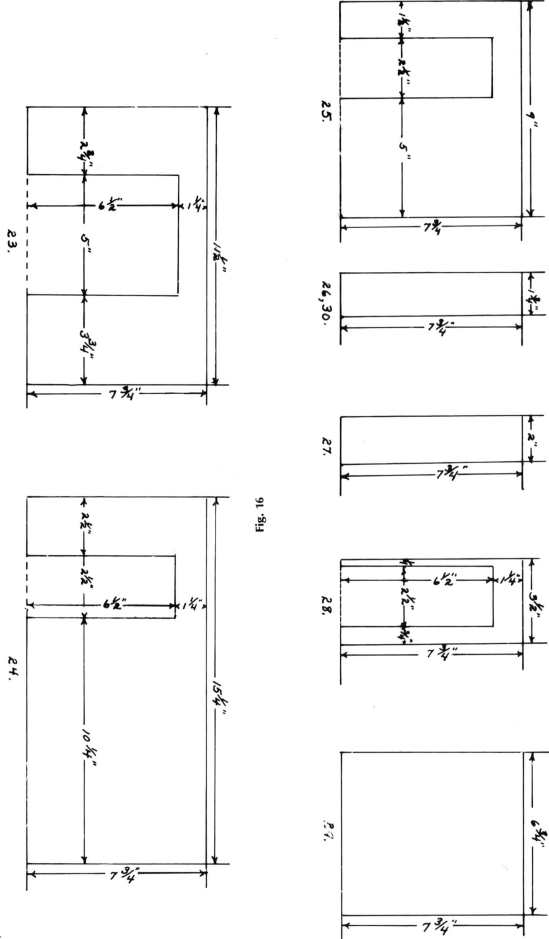

Fig. 16

Fig. 17

21. Glue and nail #19 to #20 (Fig. 18). Glue to floor. The wall partitions should be nailed, as well as glued, whenever possible.

22. Attach door #21 with small hinges at the top for access to bathroom. Glue #21 to #20 and then onto floor and wall #1.

23. Glue #25 to #26. Glue unit to #21 and floor.

24. Glue #24 to #21 and #26 and onto floor.

25. Glue #22 and #27 to both sides of #24 (as shown in Fig. 18) and onto floor and wall.

26. Glue #30 to #22 and onto floor.

27. Glue #23 to #30 and #24 and onto wall and floor.

28. Glue #18 to #27 and to #23 and onto floor.

29. Cut out two sides for second floor steps (6 3/4″ × 5 1/2″ × 1/4″) Fig. 19.

30. Cut attic stair landing 3″ × 3″ × 1/4″.

31. Glue one side of steps to wall #3 and onto second floor.

32. Glue and nail upper landing to wall at top of steps, exactly 7/16″ above the last step (Fig. 19).

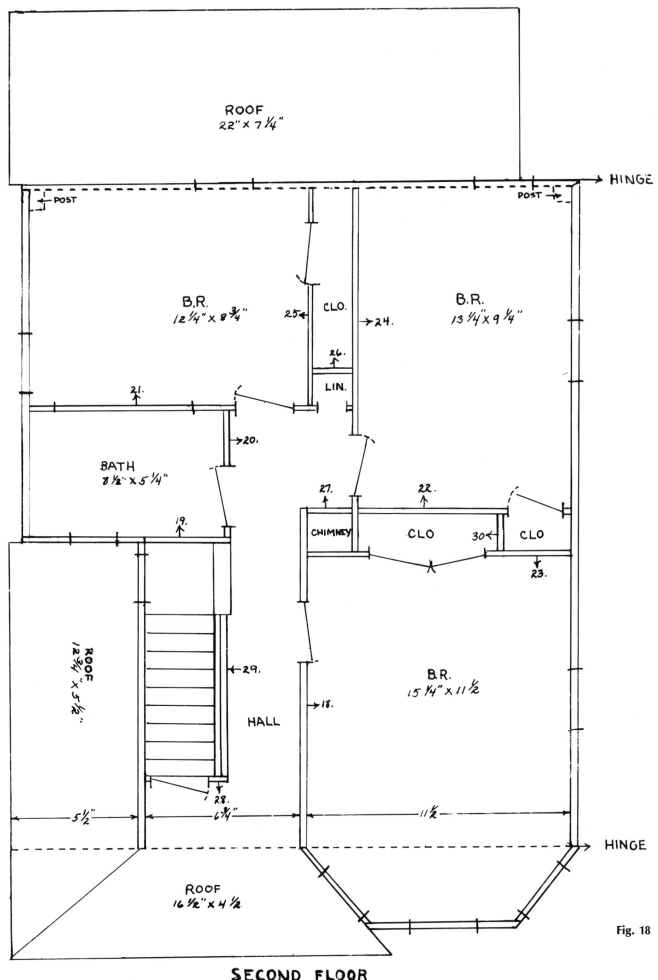

ROOF
22" X 7¼"

HINGE

POST

POST

B.R.
12¼" X 8¾"

25.← CLO. →24.

B.R.
13¼" X 9¼"

26.

LIN.

21.

20.

BATH
8½" X 5¼"

27.

22.

19.

CHIMNEY

CLO

30←

CLO

23.

ROOF
12¾" X 5½"

29.

B.R.
15¼" X 11½"

18.

HALL

28.

5½"

6¾"

11½"

HINGE

ROOF
16½" X 4½"

Fig. 18

SECOND FLOOR

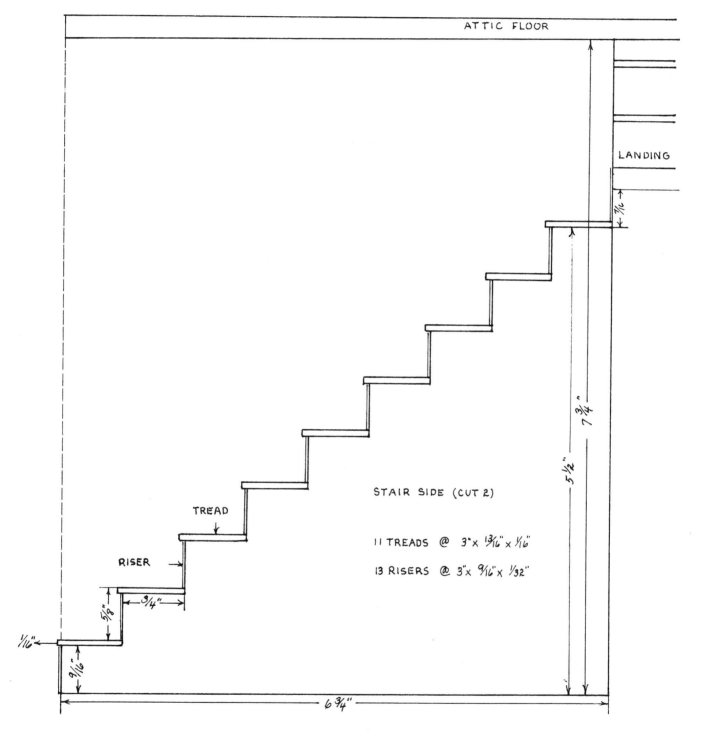

ATTIC FLOOR

LANDING

STAIR SIDE (CUT 2)

11 TREADS @ 3"x 13/16" x 1/16"

13 RISERS @ 3"x 9/16"x 1/32"

TREAD

RISER

3/4"

5/8"

1/16"

9/16"

6 3/4"

5 1/2"

7 3/4"

9/16"

SECOND FLOOR STEPS

Fig. 19

29

33. Glue other side of steps to #29 and onto second floor. The step sides should be exactly 3″ apart.

34. Cut out the third floor (attic). Note hole for steps (Fig. 20). Draw a 1″ line from the outside edge of the attic floor for roof overhang guideline. Glue and nail attic floor to the tops of the outside walls (within guideline) and onto tops of partitions.

35. Draw the floor plan of the house (without shed or bay front) onto the center section of the first floor (B, Fig. 2). Turn house upside down (onto attic floor) and glue all edges. Set house down, right side up, onto the first floor. Make sure the partitions match the drawing of the floor plan. Allow glue to set for at least one-half hour. Turn house over onto attic floor again and nail first floor to sides and partitions from underneath.

36. Glue edges of cellar sides and middle support and place house on top, making sure the front of the house is placed 7″ from the front edge of the base and 7 1/2″ from the rear edge (Fig. 1). Nail first floor to cellar at front and back edges.

37. Cut out pieces #31 through #34 (Fig. 21). The tops of #32 and #33 must be beveled to match the roof pitch (angle) in #31.

38. Draw the attic floor plan onto the attic floor (Fig. 22).

39. Glue and nail #31 to #33. Glue unit to floor.

40. Glue and nail #34 to #32. Glue unit to floor and #33.

41. Cut out step sides for the second floor upper landing, as shown in the landing detail (Fig. 12). NOTE: The last rise to the attic floor should be lowered to 5/16″ instead of 9/16″, a shorter rise than the first floor landing due to the lower ceiling.

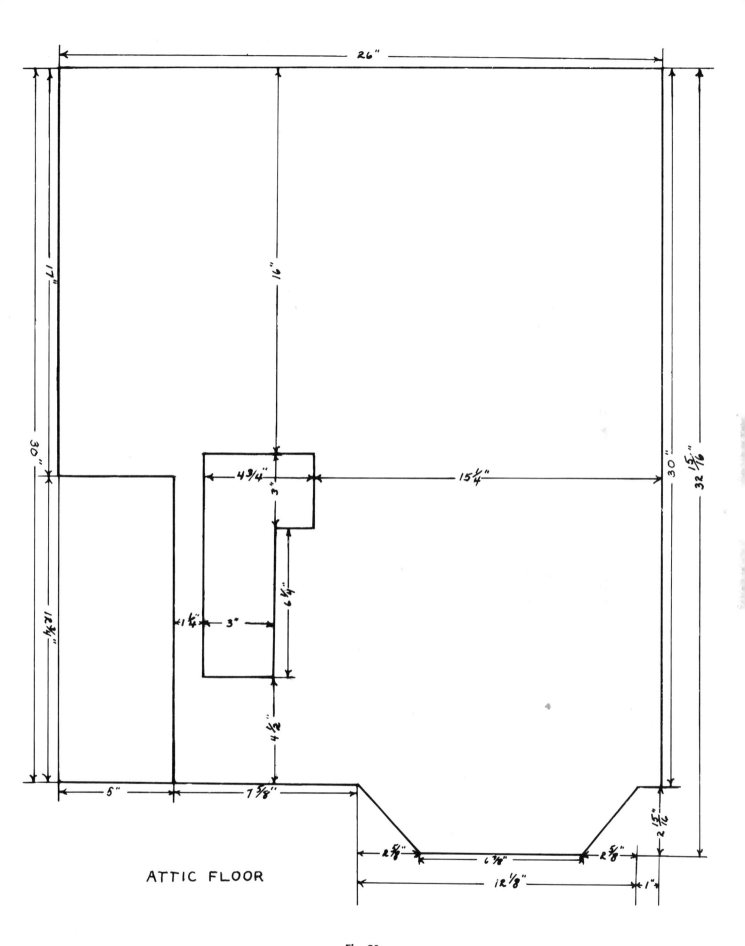

Fig. 20

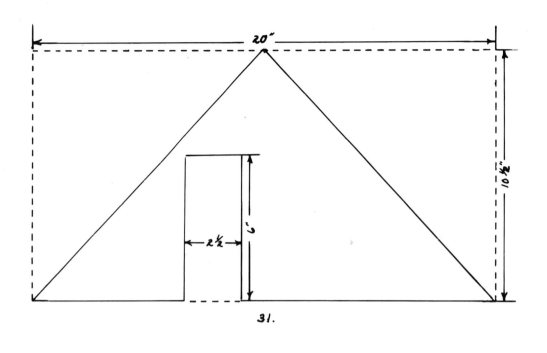

31.

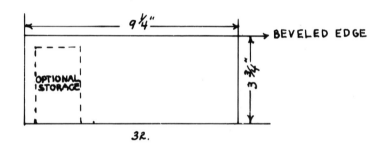

32.

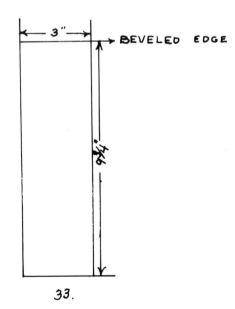

33.

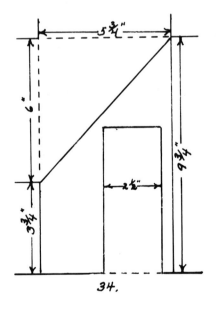

34.

Fig. 21

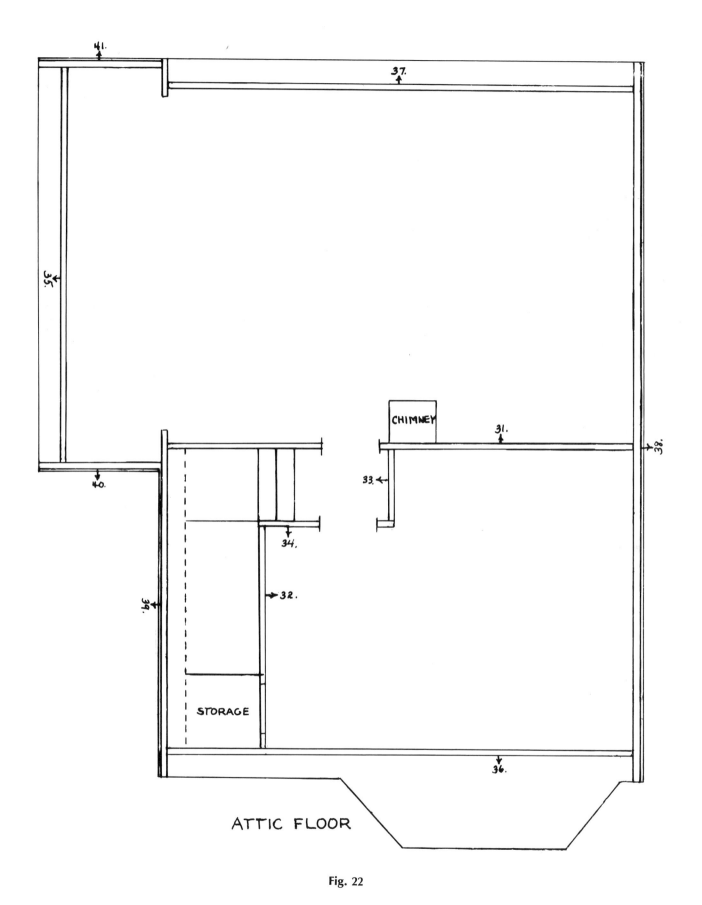

Fig. 22

42. Glue step sides for upper landing to underside of attic floor and to the landing.

43. The covers for the sides of the landing steps (Fig. 12) and covers for the underside of the steps may be added to finish the stairwells. Use 1/32″-thick bass wood or thin cardboard.

44. Glue risers and treads in place (Fig. 19). Finish with covers. Stain and carpet before roof is attached.

45. The optional (inside) attic chimney, shown in Fig. 22, measures 2″ × 1 3/4″ and is painted with white gesso or modeling paste (over mat board) to reproduce a rough plaster over brick effect. (Or just paint white with acrylic paint.) The chimney is 10 1/2″ high and the sides are cut to conform to the roof pitch shown in Fig. 21.

46. Cut out pieces #35 through #41 (Figs. 23 and 24).

47. Glue #35 1″ from edge of attic floor (Fig. 22).

48. Glue #36 and #37 1″ from edge of attic floor.

49. Attach roof-opening access door with small hinges. Glue and nail #38 to #36, #37, and #31.

50. Glue and nail #39 to #36, #37, and #31.

51. Glue and nail #40 and #41 to #35 and #39. See photos on pages 27 and 34.

52. Cut and bevel sides of chimney to conform to roof pitch (Fig. 25). Glue sides to front and back. Glue dollhouse brick paper onto chimney. (Set chimney aside until shingles are on roof.) Glue dollhouse brick paper onto cellar sides. An alternative bricking method is to score the bricks into the wood and then paint.

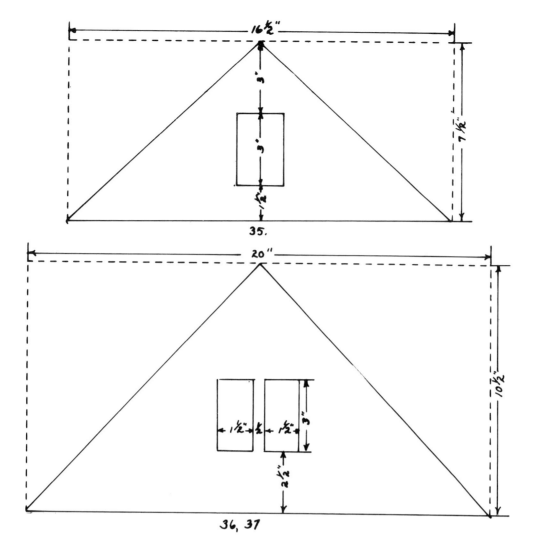

35.

36, 37

Fig. 23

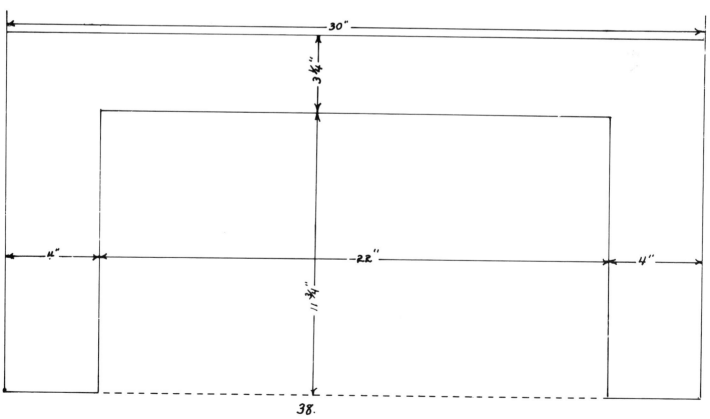

38.

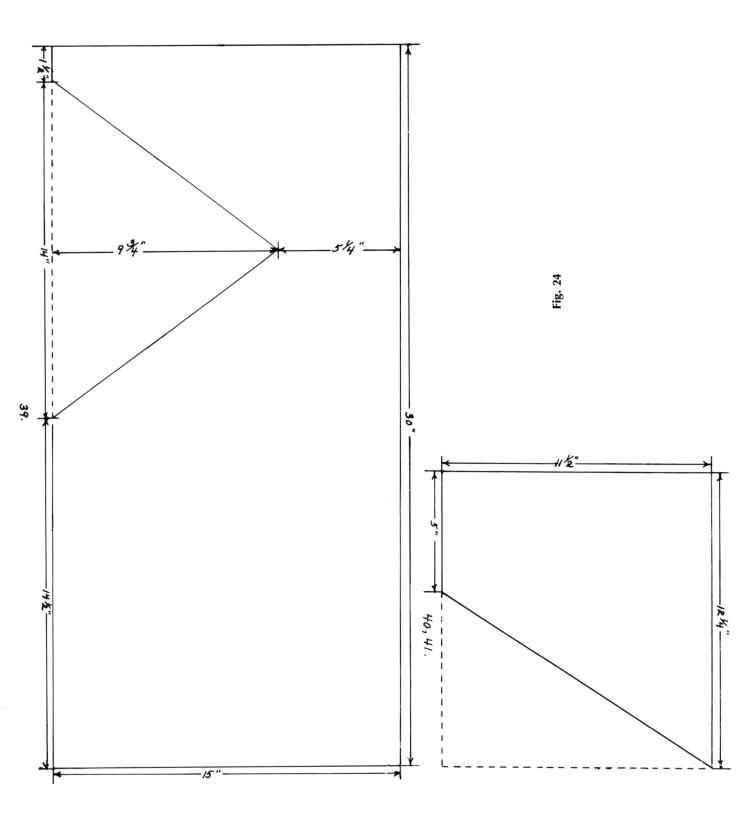

Fig. 24

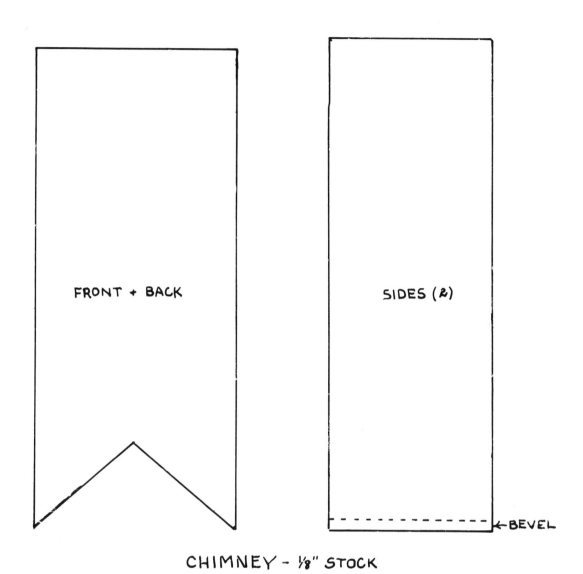

FRONT + BACK

SIDES (2)

←BEVEL

CHIMNEY - ⅛" STOCK

Fig. 25

BAY FRONT

1. Glue and nail #14 to #4 (beveled) as shown in Fig. 1.

2. Glue and nail unit to bay floor (lower section of Fig. 2).

3. Glue and nail #16 and #15 (beveled) to #14 and onto bay floor.

4. Glue and nail second bay floor to #16 and #15. (Put temporary block between floors at open end.) This step creates a storage space for out-of-season accessories and also provides an area to house a lighting system.

5. Cut porch floor supports to fill in front and sides: 15″ × 1 3/4″ × 1/4″, 3 1/2″ × 1 3/4″ × 1/4″, and 1/2″ × 1 3/4″ × 1/4″. Glue and nail porch floor supports between the two identical bay floor pieces.

6. Glue and nail upstairs bay floor B (Fig. 13) exactly eight inches above first floor bay C.

FRONT STEPS, FIG. 26
1. Cut pieces for front steps as follows:
   A. Sides, cut 2—1 7/16" × 1 1/4" × 1/4"
   B. Risers, cut 2—3 3/4" × 5/8" × 1/16"
   C. Treads, cut 2—4" × 13/16" × 1/16"
   D. Base—4" × 1 7/16" × 1/4"

2. Glue sides (A) to ends of base (D).

3. Glue risers (B) to fronts of sides (A).

4. Glue treads (C) to top of sides (A) and against risers (B).

5. Glue and nail to house (Fig. 1).

SHED
1. Glue and nail #7 to long edge of the shed floor (top portion shown in Fig. 2) exactly 1 3/4" from bottom so that the first floor of the main part of the house will be level with the shed floor (Fig. 1).

2. Glue and nail #8 and #10 to the ends of the shed floor and the ends of #7.

3. Glue and nail #9 exactly 8 1/2" from left end of shed as shown in Fig. 1.

4. Glue and nail the second shed floor piece (Fig. 2) to #7, #8, and #10 to create another storage well.

5. Bevel #6 as shown in Fig. 1. Glue and nail unit to #6.

6. Cut the shed roof 22" × 7 1/4" × 1/4". Bevel one long edge to fit against house. Glue and nail onto #6, #7, #8, #9, and #10.

SHED STEPS, FIG. 26
1. Cut pieces for two sets of shed steps as follows:
   A. Sides, cut 4—1 7/16" × 1 1/4" × 1/4"
   B. Risers, cut 4—3 1/4" × 5/8" × 1/16"
   C. Treads, cut 4—3 1/2" × 13/16" × 1/16"
   D. Base—3 1/2" × 1 7/16" × 1/4"

2. Glue two sides (A) to ends of one base piece (D).

3. Glue two risers (B) to fronts of sides (A).

4. Glue two treads (C) to top of sides (A) and against risers (B).

5. Repeat steps 2 through 4 to construct second set of shed steps.

6. Glue and nail one set of steps in front of each shed door (Fig. 1).

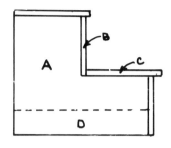

SHED AND FRONT STEPS
Fig. 26

CORNER POSTS AND HINGES
1. For added support to the rear walls, glue and nail 1/2" or 5/8" square posts between the floors and against the side walls. Placement is shown in Fig. 1 and Fig. 18. The posts also provide a more solid base to screw the piano hinges onto the house. I also decided later to add posts to the right-hand front of the house but you may not find these posts necessary.

2. Piano hinges come in different lengths. If necessary, saw the hinge with a hacksaw between the hinge springs to approximately 17 1/2" (the height of the opening is 18"). Screw one side of hinge to the bay front on outside right (#15 in Fig. 1). Lift up bay front from the base by resting it on 1/16" thick piece of wood (in closed position). Screw the other side of the piano hinge into #5 on the outside and also into the corner post.

3. Screw one side of the second hinge to the shed on the outside left (#6). Lift up shed from base by resting it on 1/16" thick piece of wood (in closed position). Screw other side of hinge into #5 on the outside and also into the corner post (if used). Saw ends of screws off if they protrude through the wood or use a shorter screw than the ones provided with the hinges.

PORCH, FIG. 27

1. Prepare the following for assembly. Identify all pieces by letter.

    A. Posts, cut 6—7″ × 3/8″ × 3/8″

    B. Balusters, cut 63—1 3/4″ × 3/16″ × 3/16″

    C-1. Railings (side porch by swing), cut 2—7 5/8″ × 3/8″ × 1/8″

    C-2. Railings (side porch to opening), cut 2—4 1/4″ × 3/8″ × 1/8″

    C-3. Railings (side opening), cut 2—3 3/8″ × 3/8″ × 1/8″

    C-4. Railings (front left), cut 2—7 1/8″ × 3/8″ × 1/8″

    C-5. Railings (front right), cut 2—1 3/4″ × 3/8″ ×1/8″

    D. Braces (under balusters), cut 6—3/8″ × 1/4″ × 1/8″

    E. Lattice frames—3/16″ square stock

    F. Lattice work—1/16″ square stock

2. Mark railings at 3/16″ intervals.

3. Lay C-1 railings on edge on flat surface 1 3/4″ apart. Lay a piece of wood 1/16″ thick, about an inch wide, and the length of the railing between the railings to rest the balusters on as they are glued. This will center the balusters between the railing edges.

4. Glue balusters between railings at 3/16″ intervals, as marked.

5. Repeat this gluing process for railings C-2, C-3, C-4, and C-5.

6. Pin and glue balustrade (balusters and railing units) to posts (A) in five sections to go around porch. The lower railing will be 1/4″ from porch floor.

7. Pin (See Furniture Construction, Pinning) and glue balustrade units 1/4″ from edge of porch floor.

8. Glue braces (D) in pairs 1/4″ apart under the lower railing as shown in photos.

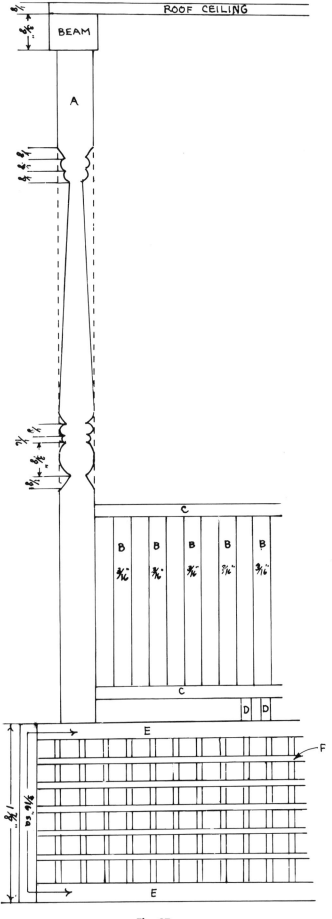

Fig. 27

40

PORCH ROOF, FIG. 28

1. Cut pieces A, B, and C. Bevel edge that goes against house as shown.

2. Cut two roof ceilings from 1/8″ stock the same size as porch floor (Fig. 1).

3. Cut three roof support beams 3/8″ × 1/2″ × 1/2″ to rest on top of posts and support roof ceiling and roof. Pin and glue to tops of posts.

4. Pin and glue roof ceiling to tops of roof support beams and to house.

5. Pin and glue roof to house and roof support beams.

PORCH LATTICE

1. Paint area under porch floor dark green or black before applying lattice work.

2. Cut lattice frames (E) to porch measurements. Cut lattice work (E) to fit inside frame, as shown in Fig. 27. Paint white on three sides.

3. Lightly mark frames into 3/16″ spaces (between lattice work).

4. Glue frames (E) to area under porch.

5. Glue lattice work (F) verticals to fit between lattice frames (E).

6. Glue lattice work (F) horizontals over vertical lattice.

CLAPBOARDS AND SHINGLES, FIG. 28

1. Cut 1/2″-wide clapboards for the house from 1/16″ plywood stock. Cut with grain.

2. Glue each length of clapboard and press onto house, always starting at bottom and allowing 1/8″ overlap. Use Tite-Bond glue. Clapboards are glued over the hinges and up to edges of windows, doors, and corners. It is a good idea to line the outside of the house into 3/8″ sections.

3. After applying a few rows of clapboards, it will be necessary to clamp (using various sizes of C-clamps) through nearby windows, doors, and corners. Clamping with an extra board over the clapboards will glue them more firmly against house.

4. Some adjustment in the width of the clapboards (plus or minus 1/2″) will have to be made at tops and bottoms of windows and doors and at the top of the house sections. Don't hurry the gluing process. It takes quite a long time with each section needing to be clamped until dry.

5. Cut the shingles for the main roof into 30″ lengths, 1″ wide, also from 1/16″ plywood stock. Cut 1/16″-wide indentations 1/2″ into the edge of the strip every 5/8″. Do this for about half of the strips needed for the roof. Cut 1/16″ wide indentations into the other half of the strips starting with 5/16″ and having 5/8″ spaces inbetween.

6. Draw 1/2″ guidelines onto roof.

7. Apply Tite-Bond glue to shingle strips and place on roof, starting at the bottom edge and alternating the two kinds of indentations cut. Overlap shingles by 1/2″.

8. Clamping under the edge of the roof and using an extra board *over* the shingles will hold the strips firmly in place until dry. An alternative to this method of shingling the house is to simply glue dollhouse shingle paper onto roof.

9. From 1/16″ stock cut 3/8″ strips for the trim on the roof, and 1″ strips for the roof cap. Glue and clamp in corners over shingles.

10. Cut 3/8″ strips from 1/16″ stock for the corner trim, edge of roof, and around the eaves. Glue and clamp into place over the clapboards.

11. Glue chimney onto roof directly above attic chimney.

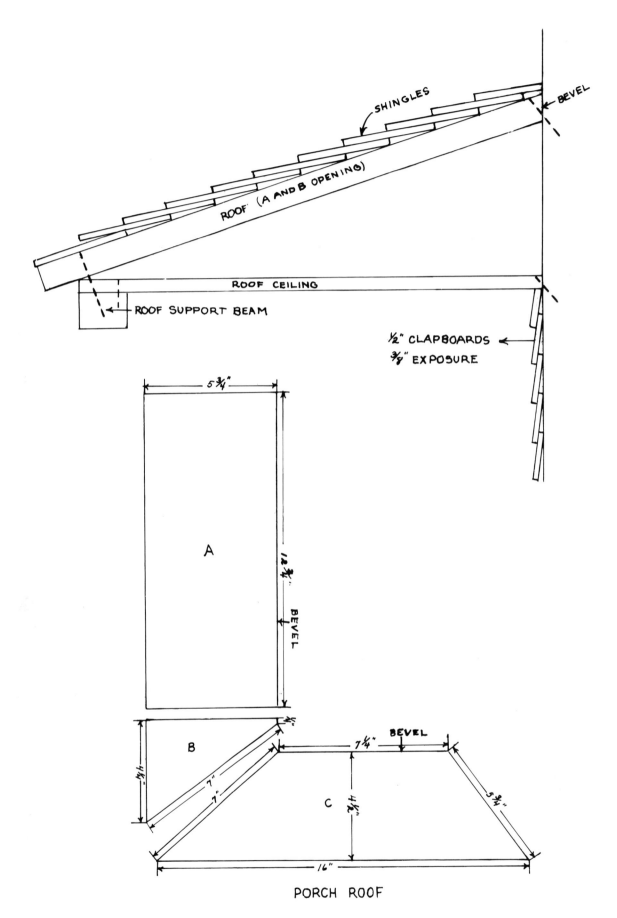

SHINGLES

BEVEL

ROOF (A AND B OPENING)

ROOF CEILING

ROOF SUPPORT BEAM

½" CLAPBOARDS
⅜" EXPOSURE

5¾"

A

12¾"

BEVEL

BEVEL

7¼"

B

4¾"

7"
7"

C

4¾"

5¾"

16"

PORCH ROOF

Fig. 28

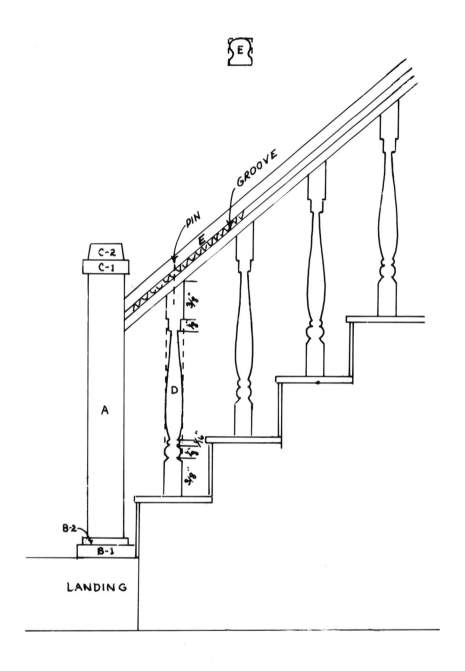

NEWEL POST AND BALUSTRADE

Fig. 29

BALUSTRADE AND NEWEL POST, FIG. 29

1. Prepare the following for assembly. Identify all pieces by letter.

A. Newel Post—2 3/4″ × 3/8″ × 3/8″
B-1. Base—5/8″ × 5/8″ × 1/8″
B-2. Base—1/2″ × 1/2″ × 1/16″
C-1. Top—1/2″ × 1/2″ × 1/8″
C-2. Top—3/8″ × 3/8″ × 3/16″
D. Balusters, cut 9—2 1/4″ × 3/16″ × 3/16″
E. Railing—9 1/8″ × 1/4″ × 1/4″

2. Glue newel post (A) to base (B-1 and B-2).

3. Glue top (C-1) to top of newel post (A) and top (C-2) to top (C-1).

4. Groove sides of railing. Mark underside of railing every 9/16″ for top of baluster placement.

5. Pin and glue balusters (D) to underside of railing. The tops of each baluster must be beveled to fit the slant of the railing.

6. Glue newel post (A) to landing.

7. Glue bottom of balusters (D) and the end of railing (E). Press firmly on treads and against newel post.

8. Stain mahogany and then varnish. (See Furniture Construction, Finishing)

WALLPAPERING AND PAINTING

Dollhouse wallpaper is available from craft shops that sell dollhouse supplies and can be ordered from dollhouse catalogs. Regular size wallpaper sample books are sometimes a good source if you can find a small, appropriate pattern. Many stores will give away old sample wallpaper books. Often these samples can be used for floor coverings as well as wallpaper. Fabric can be used for wallpaper but it has a tendency to stretch and is a little tricky to apply. Bookbinder's paper is excellent for dollhouses.

1. First, paint the ceilings white.

2. Cut the wallpaper from floor to ceiling and try not to have the patterns meet in corners. The window and door openings may be cut out before the paper is pasted or they may be cut out with an X-acto knife after the paper is hung and dry. I find that I am more successful if I cut out the holes before pasting and hanging. Try holding the paper in place and pressing the window outline on the paper to use as a cutting guide.

3. Use wallpaper paste. White glue is hard to spread and dries too rapidly. "Yes," a bookbinder's paste, is very good to use, or make your own wheat paste by mixing 3/4 cup flour with enough water to form a thin white saucelike mixture. Heat slowly in a double boiler, stirring constantly. Add small amounts of boiling water to avoid lumps. Color should be milky white. Cool.

4. Apply paste to wrong side of paper with a soft brush.

5. Smooth the paper or fabric into place with a stiffer brush or brayer (roller), moving from the center outward toward the edges, being on the lookout for wrinkles and air bubbles. If fabric is used, apply paste to wall, then lay fabric on, and smooth with a brush or roller.

6. Trim excess with an X-acto knife after the paper is dry. Don't worry if the paper doesn't go all the way to the edges of the windows, floors, or doors as the 3/8″ wood trim will cover it.

7. Paint the kitchen and bathroom walls. These walls were usually painted in the 1920s so that they could be washed. There were no exhaust fans in those days and walls became quite soiled from cooking.

8. Paint the dining room up to 6 1/4″ from the floor. Wallpaper above 6″ with matching parlor wallpaper. The plate rail will be placed at the dividing line.

9. Pine-pattern contact paper is used for the floors. Of course, you can lay real wood floor boards if preferred or paint the plywood. However, light-colored, natural floors with dark mahogany stained woodwork was typical during this period.

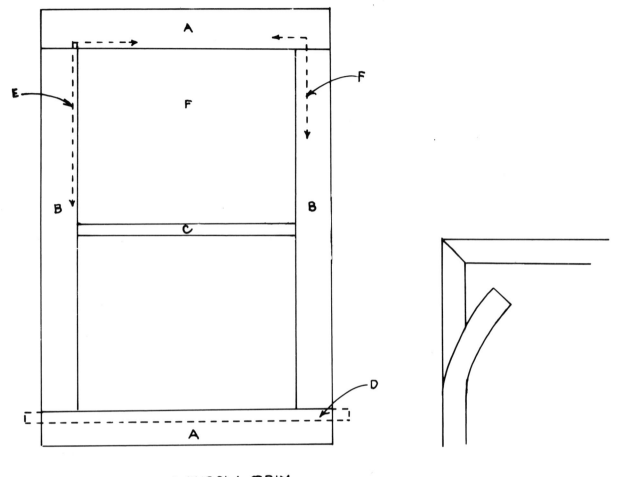

INSIDE WINDOW TRIM

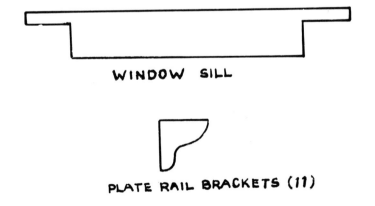

WINDOW SILL

PLATE RAIL BRACKETS (11)

Fig. 30

PLATE RAIL, FIG. 30

1. Cut and stain six lengths of 1/16" stock, 1/2" wide to circle the room between the windows and doors. Cut and stain brackets.

2. Glue brackets 6" from floor on wallpaper division, one to support each end of the longer plate rails, one to support the short section in the corner.

3. Glue shelf onto top of the brackets.

WINDOWS AND DOORS, FIG. 30

1. Cut window sills and door sills for the outside doors. Some window sills (D) will be shorter or longer than the basic pattern. Measure and adjust the length accordingly. The door sills are cut from 1/8" stock, as are the window sills, and are 1/2" wide. Measure to fit between the door sides.

2. Glue window sills with the long edge on the outside.

3. Glue door sills on the floor between the door sides.

4. Cut 1/4"-wide strips from 1/16" plywood (E) to glue around the inside edges of the window and door openings which will finish the rough-cut plywood. Do the sides first, then the top. Paint the sills and the inside frame white.

5. The "glass" (F) for the windows and doors is medium-weight clear plastic (acetate) which can be purchased in most craft shops. Cut the acetate at least 1/8" larger than the hole.

6. Apply a light coat of Quik glue around the edge of window openings *inside* the house.

7. Press acetate to window opening and press in position until it holds.

8. Cut 3/8" wide strips of 1/16" plywood to cover the acetate edge and frame the windows and doors on the inside. The framing strips (A, B) may be mitered at a 45-degree angle or may be cut straight.

9. Paint or stain.

10. Glue strips with Quik and press firmly into place around windows and doors. Sometimes it is helpful to prop a piece of wood against window with a weight behind until the glue sets.

11. Cut 1/8"-square pieces of bass wood (C) the width of the windows (for the division between the panes). Paint white on all sides.

12. Glue the dividers with Quik to the middle of the *outside* of the window.

13. Frame the outside of the windows as you did on the inside. Staining or painting on the outside may be done later.

14. Frame the doors the same as the windows, both inside and out.

METROPOLE FRONT DOOR, FIG. 31

1. Prepare the following for assembly. Identify all pieces by letter.
  A. Door, Cut 2—6 1/16" × 2 7/8" × 1/16" bass wood
  B. Mylar paper—3 1/4" × 2 1/8"
  C. Panels, cut 6— 1 7/8" × 1/2" × 1/16"
  D. Knob: 2-way commercial dollhouse knob

2. Cut one hole 3" × 1 7/8" for the "frosted glass" in each door piece.

3. Trace the door design onto the frosty side of the Mylar (B) with a sharp pencil.

4. Glue the Mylar (B) between the two sections of the door.

5. Bevel panels (C) toward outside edges, as shown.

6. Glue panels (C) onto both sides of door.

7. Sand edges evenly with a sanding block until the door fits smoothly into the door frame.

8. Drill hole and insert dollhouse brass knobs (D).

9. Stain both sides and edges with mahogany stain. Varnish.

10. Hang door on the right (facing front) with commercial dollhouse hinges.

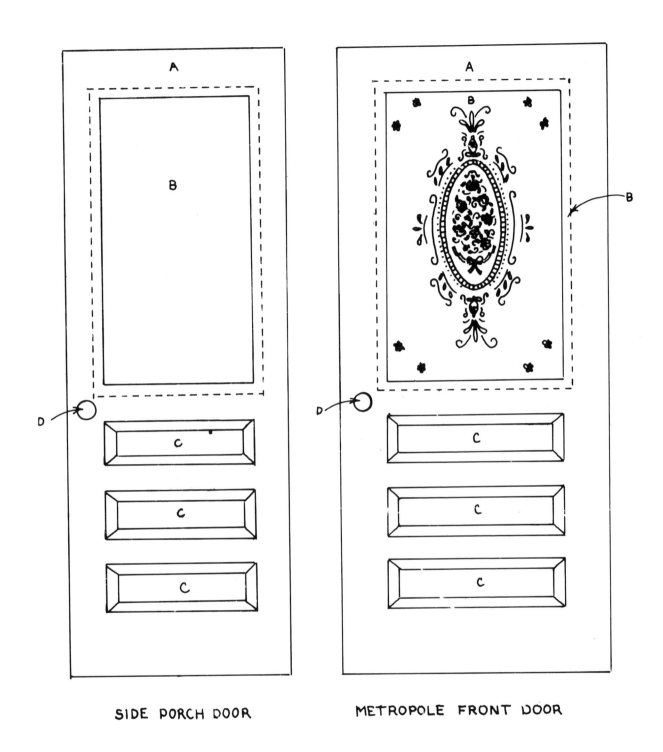

SIDE PORCH DOOR   METROPOLE FRONT DOOR

Fig. 31

SIDE PORCH DOOR, FIG. 31

1. Prepare the following for assembly. Identify all pieces by letter.
   A. Door, cut 2—6 9/16″ × 2 3/8″ × 1/16″ bass wood
   B. Clear acetate—3 1/4″ × 1 7/8″
   C. Panels, cut 6—1 5/8″ × 1/2″ × 1/16″
   D. Knob—two-way commercial dollhouse knob

2. The side porch door is constructed like the Metropole front door except that clear acetate is used for the glass and the door is 2 3/8″ wide.

SHED DOORS, FIG. 32

1. Prepare the following for assembly. Identify all pieces by letter.
   A. Doors, cut 2—6 3/8″ × 2 3/8″ × 1/16″ bass wood
   B. Acetate—3 1/4″ × 1 7/8″
   C. Panels, cut 4—1 5/8″ × 3/4″ × 1/16″
   D. Knob—two-way commercial dollhouse knob

2. The shed door going into the kitchen side is constructed like the Metropole front and side porch doors.

3. The shed door going into the laundry area is a solid piece of 1/8″ thick bass wood, the same size as the other shed door but the panels are scored into the wood with an awl. To darken the groove, a hard lead pencil may be used for scoring. This creates a satisfactory illusion but wood panels may be preferred.

4. Paint both shed doors white.

ATTIC AND INSIDE DOORS, FIG. 32

1. Cut attic and inside doors 6 3/8″ × 2 3/8″ × 1 1/16″ bass wood.

2. They are made like the solid-paneled shed door except that they are stained. I did not install inside doors so that the house would be more open for photographing purposes. Perhaps at a later date I'll add more doors, hang clothes in the closets, etc.

PAINTING

1. Spray the brick paper with an acrylic spray.

2. The attic, storage areas, and shed are stained with Puritan Pine Min-Wax. Paint if preferred.

3. The clapboards and shingles are painted with acrylic water-base paint. Paint the white trim first with two coats.

4. Masking the trim before painting the clapboards may be helpful. However, I painted the clapboards without masking, then retouched any paint overlaps. The clapboard color is a soft gray-green (add a little black and green to the white).

5. The shingles color is a darker green-gray (add more black and a lot more green). Use a small brush to get into all the crevices, then paint the tops of the shingles. Two coats will be necessary.

6. Paint the porch floor and steps with gray enamel.

7. The house base is painted a compatible green and, to add texture, sprinkle "Life-Like" grass over the surface, using a decoupage spray adhesive. An alternative "grass" is 3M flint paper (medium sandpaper) painted green.

8. Measure and cut 3M coarse emery cloth for the black tar paper on the house roof overhang. Glue in place.

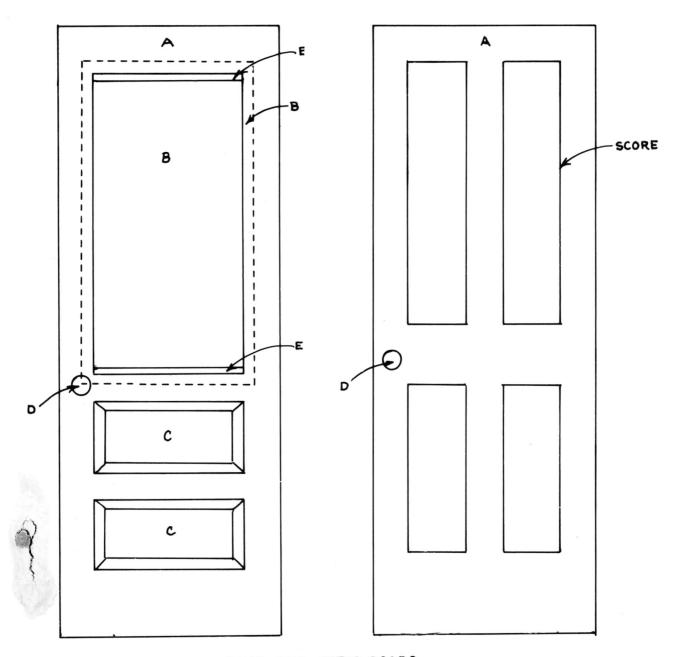

SHED AND ATTIC DOORS

Fig. 32

Furniture Construction

TOOLS

Many of the basic tools listed below can probably be found in your home. Some miniature equipment will probably have to be purchased. I found that I needed more sophisticated tools when I started using woods harder than balsa. However, everything in the dollhouse can be constructed from balsa and, if you are a beginner, I recommend starting with this soft wood.

TOOL LIST FOR BALSA WOOD

Metal-edged ruler (a metal, cork-backed ruler is recommended)
X-acto knife handle #1 or #2 or a Stanley knife (if you have one)
X-acto blades #11
Cutting board
Tweezers
Small, round, jeweler's file (to make holes in balsa and shape legs)
Miter box (not absolutely necessary but very helpful)
Miniclamps (snap clothespins, rubber bands, hair clips, or U clamps)

TOOL LIST FOR WOODS HARDER THAN BALSA

If you are an advanced beginner and not just starting your adventures in mini-land, you may want to furnish your dollhouse with harder wood pieces. Additional tools are required for working with pine, bass, and hard woods.
Hand saw (X-acto, jeweler's coping saw, or Atlas snap saw)
Jig saw (optional)
Small hand drill and assortment of bits (X-acto pin drill)
Various shaped files (optional)
Small T-square*
Calipers*
Sequin pins
Small hammer
Plastic angles (30, 45, 60, and 90 degrees) and plastic protractor*
Many craftsmen use dentists' and jewelers' equipment for constructing miniature furniture. Dremel sells an entire line of tools that can be used in miniature work. The Dremel Moto-Shop will saw, sand, and polish, and has a flexible-shaft tool with attachments. I invested in the X-acto miter box with a saw and an assortment of X-acto knife blades which fit into several size handles. A miniature lathe is made by Dremel but I do all my wood turnings by hand, simply because it gives me more satisfaction.

Although many people hand-saw hard woods, it is a tedious job and one which I soon gave up. I purchased a small hobby jig saw from Sears and now I wonder how I got along without it. A hand drill is another necessary tool when working with woods harder than balsa. By using a hand drill, furniture pieces can be joined with dowel joints. This method of construction is sturdier than butting and gluing pieces together, particularly when connecting parts such as chair rungs. However, if you choose to use dowel joints or other types of jointing, the pattern pieces in this book must be adjusted to accommodate the extra length that is necessary to form the connecting parts.

MISCELLANEOUS
Emery boards
Carbon or tracing paper (if you decide to trace the patterns)
Pencil, medium hard with a sharp point for accurate measurements
Sandpaper: 320–400 grit (Tri-Mite) garnet paper is excellent
Steel wool: 0–0000
White Glue: such as Elmer's or Sobo
Stain: acrylic stains (water-base and fast-drying), Min-wax, or other varieties that contain a sealer
Varnish: Val-oil, decoupage finish, or an acrylic varnish
Wood: balsa, pine, bass, or plywoods (for an opaque finish)
"Found" treasures: wood cigar boxes, tongue depressors, swab sticks, toothpicks, lollipop sticks, wooden meat skewers, cocktail picks
Cheesecloth
Scissors
Wood block (for sanding)
Small paint brushes, #8, #10
Small wire-cutting pliers
Needle-nose pliers

*Helpful when designing your own pieces.

The patterns in this book may be used interchangeably with balsa or other woods, as long as the wood is the thickness called for in the pattern. Balsa wood is a lightweight wood used by miniature enthusiasts because of the ease with which it can be cut and shaped. You must be gentle with it but it is relatively strong. When purchasing balsa, try to choose those pieces that have tan or brown flecks throughout the length. Avoid those with a pure white color or those that seem unusually soft. Craft stores and art and hobby shops carry a large selection of balsa sizes. The color, softness, pattern of the grain, length, width, and thickness of the wood are things to keep in mind when choosing your pieces. Balsa is commonly available in the following sizes: Length, 36" (sometimes it is packaged in shorter lengths); Widths, 1/8", 3/8", 1/4", 1/2", 1", 3", 4", 6"; Thicknesses, 1/32", 1/16", 3/32", 1/8", 1/4", 1/2", 1", 2"; Square strips, 1/16", 3/32", 1/8", 3/16", 1/4", 1/2". For the following patterns balsa 36" × 4" is recommended, in the thicknesses designated.

The furniture is scaled one inch to the foot. This is the most popular scale used by miniaturists, although many people prefer working with a larger, or even smaller, scale.

Since scale is of the utmost importance in the construction of miniatures, the selection of the wood to be used is of primary concern. Color, uniformity of the grain pattern, strength, and ease in handling should be considered in light of the piece to be constructed. Fine-grained woods are generally desirable. Veneers can often be used. Bass and pine woods are excellent choices and both can be stained effectively to look like other woods. Small woodworking shops will usually accommodate requests for specially milled lumber. Some larger lumber yards carry a limited supply of stock suitable for miniature furniture construction. Craft stores and art and hobby shops sometimes carry bass wood as well as balsa wood. Look in the *Yellow Pages* to find other local sources.

BASIC TECHNIQUES
DESIGNING FURNITURE
If you design your own furniture, you should have a ruler calibrated to various scales (e.g., 1" = 1', 1/2" = 1'). A ruler of this type, usually triangular in shape, and a small T square, calipers, plastic angles, and a protractor can be purchased at office supply stores. These items are inexpensive and will be of invaluable help for accurate measurements. Measure carefully the item you want to reproduce in miniature. Draw patterns to *scale* of the various pieces that will be joined together. Use a fine drawing point. You will find that making cardboard or mat-board models, of the same thickness wood you will be using, will help ensure that the pieces will fit together properly. Working plans (blueprints) of various styles and periods of furniture are available in your library.

TRANSFERRING PATTERNS
The patterns can be transferred to the wood by using tracing paper or carbon paper. You may also cut the pattern out and draw or cut around it. A drop of rubber cement will hold the pattern in place and will not stain the wood. I prefer to draw directly onto the wood because it is more precise than tracing. All of the patterns in this book are scaled to size. A small T square or plastic angles are helpful when drawing directly onto the wood.

CUTTING BALSA
It is important when cutting balsa or other thin wood to hold the knife perpendicular to the wood so that the edges will not be angled and will match flush when they are joined together. To cut straight lines, place a metal-edged ruler (as a guide for the knife) on the line to be cut, drawing the blade slowly along the line. Do not use too much pressure or the wood will crush. It is better to make several cuts until you can feel the blade go completely through the wood. Cut the *cross* grain first. (The fibers will run in the direction of the grain.) It is much easier to cut *with* the grain but there is some danger of the wood splitting. Use the same piece of wood for the entire piece of furniture so the grain and the color will be consistent. Make sure you cut the pattern so that the grain is running in the right direction, for strength as well as authenticity. (Think of the "board" construction of the piece you are reproducing.) This is not so important if a piece is made of plywood or if it is to be painted. If you decide to cut (or saw) individual boards for the construction, instead of scoring the wood to simulate boards, it is advisable to cut or saw all the boards from the same piece of wood in the order that they will be joined together. The boards will then fit together perfectly without cracks. Cut slightly beyond the point where corners meet so as to keep them sharp. Always use a cutting board to prevent marking surfaces underneath your work.

SANDING
Sanding is undertaken throughout the various stages of construction to refine the wood surface. A fine sandpaper is usually applied first and then fine steel wool to achieve a smooth finished surface. Sand lightly, using a wood block covered with sandpaper for flat surfaces. Always sand with the grain direction. An emery board is useful for inside corners and smoothing turned posts.

SHAPING A LEG OR POST
Both square and round wood (dowel) can be used for posts, whichever seems to lend itself better to the turnings. Balsa and bass squares are available. Make a pencil mark where the turning is to be across all sides of a square piece of wood or around a dowel where the pattern indicates, making the ends meet. Cut gently into the line, if using a knife instead of a jeweler's file, for the indentations. Hold the blade perpendicular to the wood until the piece is circled. Then cut at an angle to meet the first line cut so that the chip will fall away. Do not cut too deeply. It is easier to make indentations with various sizes and shapes of jewelers' files but I like to do my initial carving with a knife, as I did for the pieces in this dollhouse. Square pieces may be filed all at one time for uniformity, by holding or taping the pieces together as a single block. Trim off the square corners that need to be rounded and the round corners that need to be squared. Taper with a knife where indicated (lower legs) on the patterns. Sand on a

sandpaper block by twisting or turning the leg or post. Sand the roughly shaped pieces with emery boards or small strips of emery cloth held around the indentation while turning the leg or post. Curves can also be sanded by wrapping sandpaper around a pencil or dowel that matches the size of the curve.

PINNING

This procedure provides extra strength. First cut off and discard about one-third of a pin, including the head. The pin will fly so this should be done inside a large paper bag. Dip one end of the pin into glue and insert it half-way into the top of the piece. A hole may have to be drilled (see cutting holes in wood below) into the piece before the pin can be inserted. Balsa wood is soft enough to allow the pin to be placed by hand. Dip the other half of the pin into glue, glue the top surface of the connecting part, and insert the pin into the bottom of the piece to be joined. Be sure that the pin is straight when it is inserted.

SCORING

Scoring means to cut or indent a groove part-way into a solid surface. Scoring mat board or cardboard part-way with a knife will enable you to bend it precisely along a straight line. When using a dull pencil to score wood, the groove will be darkened and give the piece a paneled effect or a cut-board effect. X-acto knives have special blades for cutting grooves into wood.

CUTTING HOLES IN WOOD

The easiest way to cut a round hole in balsa wood is to rotate a circular jeweler's file into the wood. Holes in harder wood will have to be drilled with a hand or electric drill, using the correct size bits. (A vise is necessary to hold the piece.) Square or oblong holes are cut with a knife, cross grain first and slightly smaller than indicated on the patterns. Sand the hole with an appropriate size emery board.

BENDING WOOD

Wood has to be softened for bending and then allowed to dry in the desired shape. Soak the wood to be bent in a solution of three parts water to one part ammonia. (Sometimes just soaking it in hot water will be sufficient, depending on the piece and how much it has to be bent.) Be sure the wood is weighted down or taped so that it is immersed and will absorb the water. Soak overnight or until the wood is easily bent. Bend around a form (cans, jars, dowels) that duplicates the desired curve. Tape the wood to the form and allow to dry thoroughly. The color will lighten as it dries.

JOINTING

Jointing refers to how parts are fastened together. Some miniaturists join their pieces by dovetailing, dowel pinning, or tongue and groove. Since I'm not a purist, I use the butt jointing process (solid end flush against solid end) because it is so simple and usually effective for miniature furniture, particularly if joining balsa wood. Harder woods can be reinforced after gluing by using sequin pins for

nails where the pieces join. Sequin pins are short straight pins that are used to attach sequins to art objects. They are available in most craft shops. The pin is inserted part-way, the head of the pin is cut off with cutting pliers, and then the remaining shaft is driven in the rest of the way. Remember, the pin head will fly when cut so the procedure should be done inside a large paper bag. The pin may be set farther into the wood with a small nail punch and the hole covered with a wood crayon (found in different wood colors in hardware stores). The patterns in this book are all designed for butt jointing.

MITERING

Mitering is the junction of two pieces of wood at an angle, usually 45 degrees. Picture frames as well as door and window molding are usually mitered at the corners. The X-acto miter box has a straight cut (good for sawing dowels and lengths of wood for legs and such) and two cuts for the opposite 45-degree angles. Place the saw in the desired cut and draw the saw gently toward you. Hold saw handle at the very end and do not bear down. Repeat this backward motion if necessary. Be careful when sawing back and forth or the wood may splinter. There is a lip on the front edge of my miter box to keep it from slipping. If you do not have a plastic angle or miter box, a piece of paper (typing paper is cut at a 90 degree angle) can be folded to get a 45 degree angle. With the piece of paper flat in front of you, fold so that the top edge of the paper runs parallel to the left side of the paper. The folded crease will form a 45 degree angle and can be traced onto the wood you want to cut.

MAKING A DRAWER

There are two types of drawer fronts that can be used: The front of a drawer can either fit flush with the front of the piece or can be slightly larger than the hole in which the drawer fits so that the lip acts as a drawer stop. The depth of the drawer must be measured exactly so that the drawer will go all the way to the back of the piece. If not, a drawer stop must be provided.

Use 1/16" stock for the back of the drawer construction. The sides and back rest on the drawer bottom with the side pieces fitted between the front and back pieces. The sides and back should be cut slightly lower than the top of the drawer opening. Drawers have to rest on something, and I have used both runners (strips of wood) and a solid piece of wood to support them. Both are authentic and easy procedures if your measuring is accurate.

Drawer pulls can be made out of slices of pine dowels, pin or nail heads, beads, or shaped from "Sculpey" clay. The pin or nail can be hammered or pushed through the drawer front, the shank clipped in back, and held in place with a spot of glue where it has been clipped. Dowel slices and clay pulls glued in place will be secure enough to allow the drawer to be opened and closed.

GLUING

I prefer to glue pieces together *before* staining because some corrective sanding may need to be done after gluing and it is very difficult to "touch up" sanded spots with stain. However, this must be done very carefully so that glue is not squeezed out around the joining pieces. Only a very small amount of glue is necessary to hold a unit together. If the glue gets on a part to be stained, wipe it off with a damp cloth and sand over the spot. (Glue is absorbed into the wood and "seals" it so that it will not take the color of a subsequent stain.) Sometimes it is necessary to use miniclamps (see tool list for balsa wood) or weights to hold pieces together to prevent warping until they are dry. Consider carefully the *order* in which the parts are to be glued together. For instance, a headboard for a bed should be glued separately from the footboard and allowed to dry before the side pieces (rails) are attached. It is a good idea to glue pieces together on wax paper so that excess glue will not adhere the piece to your working surface. (I have glued pieces to my cutting board without realizing it.)

STAINING

Wood stains may be applied with a brush or wiped on with a piece of cloth. (Cheesecloth is best because it is lint-free). Most stains act as a partial sealer. All wood surfaces require sealing. Wood is porous so the little holes in the wood have to be filled to achieve a smooth impregnable surface. Many sealers, particularly stains, will raise the grain in wood (especially balsa) and necessitate light sanding with steel wool. If you stain the parts of a unit *before* gluing them together to avoid glue spots, stain the edges as well as the flat surfaces. Lay the pieces flat to dry so the stain will not run or streak. Wipe with a piece of cheesecloth if the stain is too dark, or wet the cheesecloth in the solvent for the stain and then wipe some of the color away. Allow to dry thoroughly before the varnish or final finish is applied. Stains are available in pine, fruitwood, cherry, maple, walnut, and mahogany, as well as less-known wood colors. I recommend using acrylic stains because they are water-based, fast drying, and are available in small quantities (usually two- and four-ounce quantities) at craft and hobby shops.

FINISHING

Val-oil is a combination of oil and varnish and can be used as a final finishing coat as well as a sealer. Each succeeding coat must be sanded lightly with steel wool until the surface is smooth. I like Val-oil because it *penetrates* and seals wood (*after* it is stained the desired shade). Apply Val-oil before painting a balsa piece an opaque color (to strengthen the wood) because paint has a tendency to stay on top of the wood and is not absorbed. There are various stains, colors, and sealers on the market, such as orange or clear shellac, linseed oil, lacquer, wax, opaque colors, and the newer finishes like acrylic, vinyl, or polyurethane. Usually two coats are required to achieve a smooth durable finish. Remember, never use a finish before staining. Remember also that you can put varnish or enamel over lacquer, but never lacquer over paint or varnish.

Lacquer will blister whatever finish it covers. Use water to thin water-based paints and acrylic stains. Water-based finishes are odorless, fast-drying, and easy to clean up after use. Oil-based finishes and varnish require turpentine for thinning and clean-up. Thin shellac with alcohol. The product's label will tell you if the paint or finish you want to use is water-based or not. It is not a good idea to use regular watercolors because they sometimes run when the finishing coat is applied. Decoupage finish (aerosol or brush-on) can be used for final finishing. Colorless fingernail polish supplies a high gloss finish for the ceramic pieces. Keep in mind the type of gloss you prefer when choosing varnish for your finishing coat. Varnish can be used over paint or stain for the final coat as long as it is compatible with the base treatment.

Antiquing is another type of finishing that is very effective for miniature furniture. An antiquing glaze of your color choice can be purchased in small amounts. The glaze is applied over a base paint and then quickly wiped off to let the base color show through. A lint-free cloth, such as cheesecloth, should be used to wipe the glaze. Wipe gently in the direction of the grain and do not wipe too much of the glaze off or you will lose the antique effect. The glaze will stay in corners and cracks and will enhance the antique quality you want to create. Decoupage finish or varnish can be used for the final sealer coat. Always check to see if the finishes you apply are compatible with each other (for instance, use a water-base finish over a water-base paint). Hand-painted decorative finishes should always be protected with a final coat of varnish or plastic spray.

HINGING

Hinges can be simulated by using cheesecloth, fine fabric, or typing paper. Typing paper of good quality is just as strong as a cloth hinge and usually my preference. If hinges are to be used for a box shape with a lid, rather than a door where the exposed hinge is covered with molding, the application is somewhat different. In this case the hinge has to be glued to the underside of the lid (instead of between layers of wood), the back edge of the box unit, and then into the inside of the box. The fabric or paper is folded between the edges of the pieces to be joined. Hinges should be measured 1/4" short of the top and bottom of a piece and should be about 5/8" wide. Box hinges may be used in pairs, one on each side of the lid, and should be small in comparison to the piece. Strap hinges (see six-board chest pattern) may be made from fabric, small pieces of thin leather, or, again, typing paper. Strap hinges and butterfly hinges were used extensively during the Colonial period. These hinges are glued to the *outside* of the two pieces you wish to join. Always glue strap hinges with the lid in a closed position. Commercial dollhouse hinges are now available if you prefer to make this investment. They may be attached with sequin pins.

Furniture Patterns and Directions

FRONT HALL AND PARLOR

The mahogany-stained woodwork throughout the house is particularly handsome in the front hall. The newel post, balustrade, and all the brass door knobs in the house customarily got a weekly polish.

The oval mirror at the foot of the steps is conveniently placed for full-length viewing.

Teenagers, then as now, monopolized the front-hall phone for hours on end. (It was hung on the other side of the parlor arch but I moved it forward so that it could be seen more easily.)

The umbrella stand holds Grandfather's cane and Father Jellison's umbrella.

A hall rack (chair and coat-rack combination) with storage for boots in the hutch seat, was a common, practical furniture item in the days before front halls had coat closets.

The upright mahogany piano, situated under the long, high piano window, fairly dominates the parlor. The family Bible rests on the crocheted piano drape, along with a lamp and a stereoscopic viewer.

Father's reclining Morris chair (now being reproduced at very fancy prices) provides a restful spot next to the fireplace for reading the evening paper and listening to Billy Jones and Ernie Hare on the radio, which is just around the corner in the dining room.

The massive mahogany, pillared fireplace with a mirror above the mantle is rather overwhelming, but it was then very fashionable. The mahogany trim was removed during the 1940s to reveal a simple but effective birch mantle and paneling. At the same time, the mahogany stain was removed from the woodwork throughout the rest of the house and refinished in the natural light color of the birch wood.

Green velvet tufted cushions enhance the three-piece parlor suite, newly acquired when the house was bought. It is not so comfortable, I'm afraid, as the later upholstered parlor suites of the 1930s.

The rose and green rug with fringed ends blends well with the wallpaper and green cushions on the settee set. Floral patterns were becoming popular for rugs, a change from the oriental and geometric patterns of earlier years.

The old victrola is in the corner. Charlie and Polly Jellison tell me that the rug was often rolled back in the room so that they and their friends could dance to the music of Paul Whiteman.

The inevitable Belgian lace curtains hang delicately at the windows in the parlor, as well as in the dining room. A pedestal flower stand, with a graceful fern potted in a brass container, stands in the bay window. The rope portieres between the parlor and dining room are replaced with heavy tapestries during the winter months.

Notice the ice card in the bay front window and the elegant pink crystal ceiling fixture.

HALL RACK, FIG. 33

1. Prepare the following for assembly. Identify all pieces by letter.
   A. Back—6" × 1 58" × 1/8"
   B. Seat—2" × 1 1/2" × 1/8" (cut out lift top)
   C. Seat front—1 3/4" × 3/4" × 1/8"
   D. Seat sides, cut 2—1 1/2" × 1/2" × 1/8"
   E. Seat bottom—1 3/4" × 1 3/8" × 1/8"
   F. Arms, cut 2—1 3/4" × 1/2" × 1/8"
   G. Front legs, cut 2—2 1/4" × 3/8" × 1/8"

2. Score or gouge design on back (A) and seat front (C).

3. Hinge seat (B) to bottom (See Furniture Construction, Hinges).

4. Glue bottom (E) between seat sides (D).

5. Glue seat front (C) between sides (D) and onto bottom edge (E).

6. Glue and pin seat unit to back (A) exactly 1 1/2" from floor. (See Furniture Construction, Pinning)

7. Glue and pin front legs (G) to seat unit.

8. Glue and pin arms (F) to back (A) and front legs (G).

9. Shape hooks from wire. Drill holes and glue in place.

10. Glue tin mirror to back.

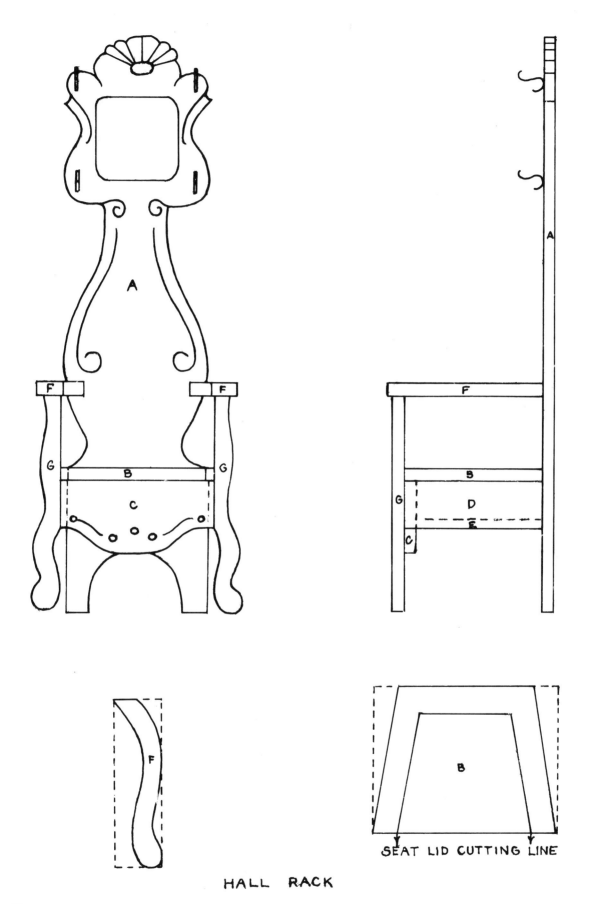

SEAT LID CUTTING LINE

HALL RACK

Fig. 33

CEILING

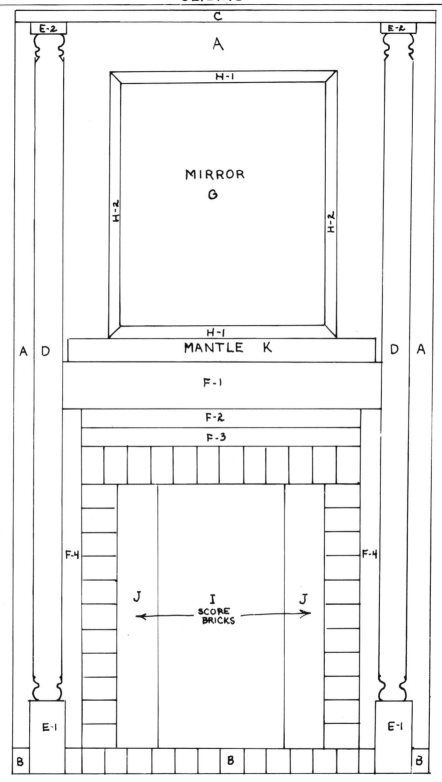

FIREPLACE

Fig. 34

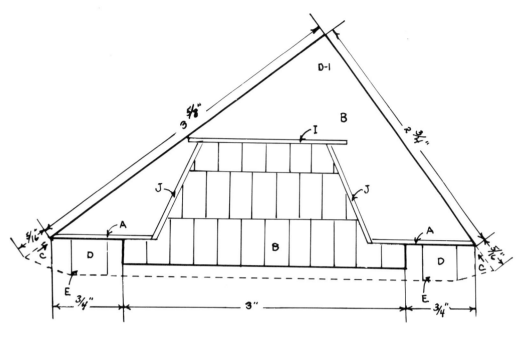

FIREPLACE BASE AND TOP

Fig. 35

FIREPLACE, FIGS. 34 AND 35

1. Prepare the following for assembly. Identify all pieces by letter.
   A. Fireplace face—7 9/16″ × 4 1/2″ × 1/16″ (opening is 2 3/4″ × 2 1/4″)
   B. Base—Cut to triangular dark line dimensions (B) on Fig. 35, 1/4″ thick stock
   C. Top—Cut to dark line on sides (as for base) and dotted line (C) on Fig. 35. 1/8″ thick stock
   D. Pillars, cut 2—6 15/16″ × 5/16″ × 5/16″ (round)
   D-1. Post support: 7 9/16″ × 5/16″ × 5/16″ (rear corner)
   E-1. Pillar bases, cut 2—3/4″ × 3/8″ × 3/8″
   E-2. Pillar tops, cut 2—3/8″ × 3/8″ × 1/8″
   F-1. Fireplace molding—2 3/8″ × 1/2″ × 1/8″
   F-2. Molding—3″ × 3/16″ × 1/16″
   F-3. Molding—3″ × 3/16″ × 1/32″
   F-4. Molding, cut 2—3 1/2″ × 3/16″ × 1/16″
   G. Mirror—2 5/8″ × 2 5/16″ tin
   H-1. Mirror frame; cut 2—2 7/16″ × 1/8″ × 1/16″
   H-2. Mirror frame; cut 2—2 3/4″ × 1/8″ × 1/16″
   I. Back wall—3 1/2″ × 1 3/4″ × 1/16″ (brick over)
   J. Side walls, cut 2—3 1/2″ × 1 1/8″ × 1/16″ (brick over)
   K. Mantle—3 5/8″ × 1/2″ × 1/4″

2. Cut opening in fireplace face (A), 2 3/4″ × 2 1/4″.

3. Score and paint bricks on face (A), hearth base (B), back wall (I), and side walls (J). Or use brick dollhouse paper.

4. Glue pillar bases (E-1) and pillar tops (E-2) to pillars (D).

5. Glue fireplace molding F-1, F-2, F-3, F-4, to fireplace face (A) as shown.

6. Glue mantle (K) to fireplace face (A).

7. Glue mirror (G) to fireplace face (A) and glue frame (H-1, H-2) around mirror.

8. Glue post support (D-1) to base (B) at rear corner of fireplace.

9. Glue pillar units to fireplace face (A).

10. Glue finished unit (A) to base (B). Prop up if necessary.

11. Glue top (C) to pillars and post (D-1) and face unit (A).

12. Glue back wall (I) and side walls (J) to base (B) and to each other as shown.

13. Stain mahogany and varnish with a high gloss.

SETTEE AND SIDE CHAIRS, FIG. 36

1. Prepare the following for assembly. Identify all pieces by letter.
  A. Settee Top—3 1/4″ × 3/8″ × 1/8″
  B-1. Middle slat, cut 3 (2 for chairs)—1 1/2″ × 1″ × 1/16″
  B-2. Side slats, cut 2—1 1/2″ × 5/8″ × 1/16″
  C. Settee seat—3 5/8″ × 1 1/2″ × 1/8″
  D. Arms, cut 6 (for all 3 pieces)—1 7/8″ × 1 1/8″ × 1/8″
  E. Back legs, cut 6 (for all 3 pieces)—3 1/4″ × 3/8″ × 1/8″
  F. Front legs, cut 4 (for settee and 1 chair)—2″ × 3/8″ × 1/8″
  G. Side chair tops, cut 2—1 1/2″ × 3/8″ × 1/8″
  H. Rocker front legs, cut 2—2″ × 3/8″ × 1/8″
  I. Rockers, cut 2—2 1/2″ × 1/2″ × 1/8″
  J. Side chair seats, cut 2—1 7/8″ × 1/2″ × 1/8″

2. Glue settee slats (B-1, B-2) to top (A) and seat (C).

3. Glue and pin arms (D) to back legs (E) and top (A).

4. Glue back legs (E) to seat (C).

5. Glue front legs (F) to seat (C) and under arms (D).

6. Repeat steps 2–5 for the side chair and rocker, using H and I.

7. Use seat patterns C and J for the cushions. Tuft every 1/2″.

BECKWITH PIANO, FIG. 37

1. Prepare the following for assembly. Identify all pieces by letter.
  A. Back: 4 3/4″ × 4 1/2″ × 1/8″
  B. Sides, cut 2—4 1/2″ × 1″ × 1/8″
  C. Bottom—4 3/4″ × 3/4″ × 1/8″
  D. Lower front—4 3/4″ × 3″ × 1/8″
  E. Top front panel—4 3/4″ × 1 1/2″ × 1/8″
  F. Keyboard sides, cut 2—7/8″ × 7/8″ × 1/8″
  G. Keyboard base—4 3/4″ × 3/4″ × 1/4″
  H. Board behind keys—4 3/4″ × 1/4″ × 1/8″
  I. Top of keyboard unit—5 1/4″ × 1/4″ × 1/16″
  J. Key board—4 3/4″ × 7/16″ × 1/16″
  K. Base—5 1/4″ × 1″ × 1/8″
  L. Leg base, cut 2—7/8″ × 3/8″ × 1/4″
  M. Lower leg braces, cut 2—13/16″ × 3/8″ × 1/4″
  N. Upper leg braces, cut 2—1″ × 1/4″ × 1/4″
  O. Legs, cut 2—1 1/16″ × 3/8″ × 3/8″
  P. Top—5 1/4″ × 1 1/4″ × 1/8″
  Q. Front molding—1 1/2″ × 1/8″ × 1/8″

2. Glue bottom (C) to lower front edge of back (A).

3. Glue lower front (D) to front edge of bottom (C).

4. Glue sides (B) to ends of back (A), lower front (D), and against ends of bottom (C).

5. Pin top front panel (E) to forward top of sides (B) by inserting a sequin pin into side board and into panel edge. Clip head of pin and drive remaining part all the way in. This panel is the adjustable music shelf.

6. Glue sides of keyboard unit (F) against each end of keyboard base (G).

7. Glue unit to base (K).

8. Glue board behind keys (H) to keyboard base (G).

9. Glue top of keyboard unit (I) to keyboard sides (F).

10. Cut out keyboard print and glue with rubber cement to keyboard (J). Glue covered keyboard (J) to keyboard base (G) and board behind keys (H).

11. Glue the entire keyboard assembly to the lower front (D) of the piano.

12. Center and glue lower leg braces (M) to leg base (L).

13. Glue units to each end of the lower front (D).

14. Glue upper leg braces (N) to bottom of base (K) and to lower front (D).

15. Glue legs (O) between upper (N) and lower (M) leg braces.

16. Glue shaped molding (Q) to front edge of sides (B).

17. Hinge piano top (P) to back (A). (See Furniture Construction, Hinges)

PIANO STOOL, FIG. 37

1. Prepare the following for assembly. Identify all pieces by letter.
  A. Seat—1 1/8″ diameter circle × 1/8″
  B. Seat—1 1/8″ diameter circle × 1/16″
  C. Pedestal top—3/4″ diameter circle × 1/8″
  D. Pedestal—3/8″ × 3/8″ × 1″
  E. Legs, cut 4—3/16″ dowel × 1 1/8″
  F. Bolt (flat head)—3/32″ diameter × 5/8″ long
  G. Nut—1/4″ × 3/32″ diameter hole.
  H. Rungs—4 round toothpicks 1/4″ long

2. Drill 3/32″ hole in pedestal (D).

3. Drill 3/32″ hole in pedestal top (C) and seat (A).

4. Countersink head of bolt (F) into seat (A), countersink nut (G) into pedestal (D).

5. Glue seat (B) to seat (A) which will cover the bolt head.

6. Glue and pin legs (E) to pedestal top (C).

7. Glue rungs (H) to pedestal (D) and legs (E).

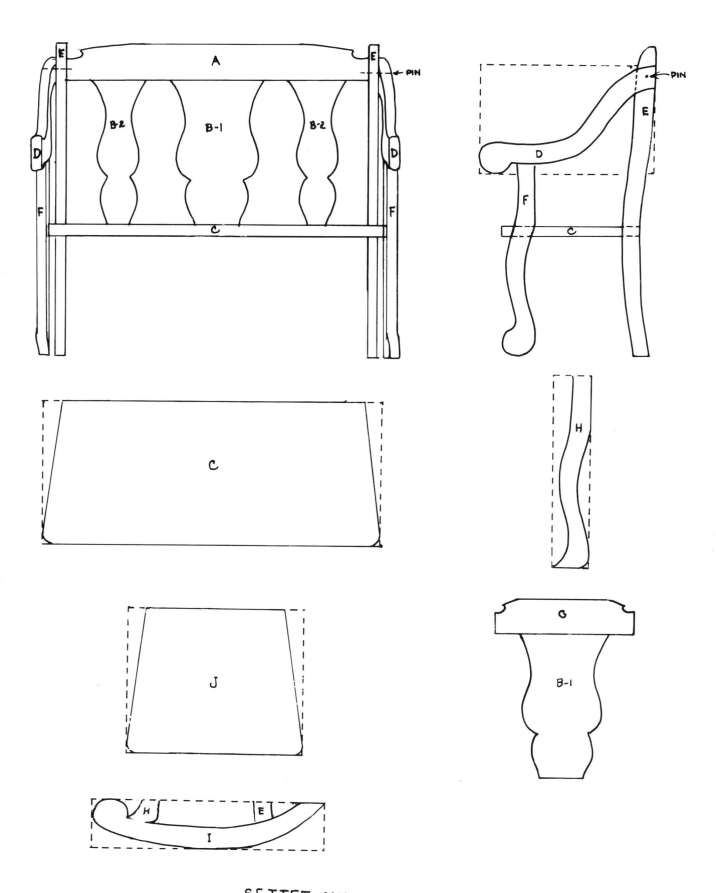

Fig. 36

SETTEE AND SIDE CHAIRS

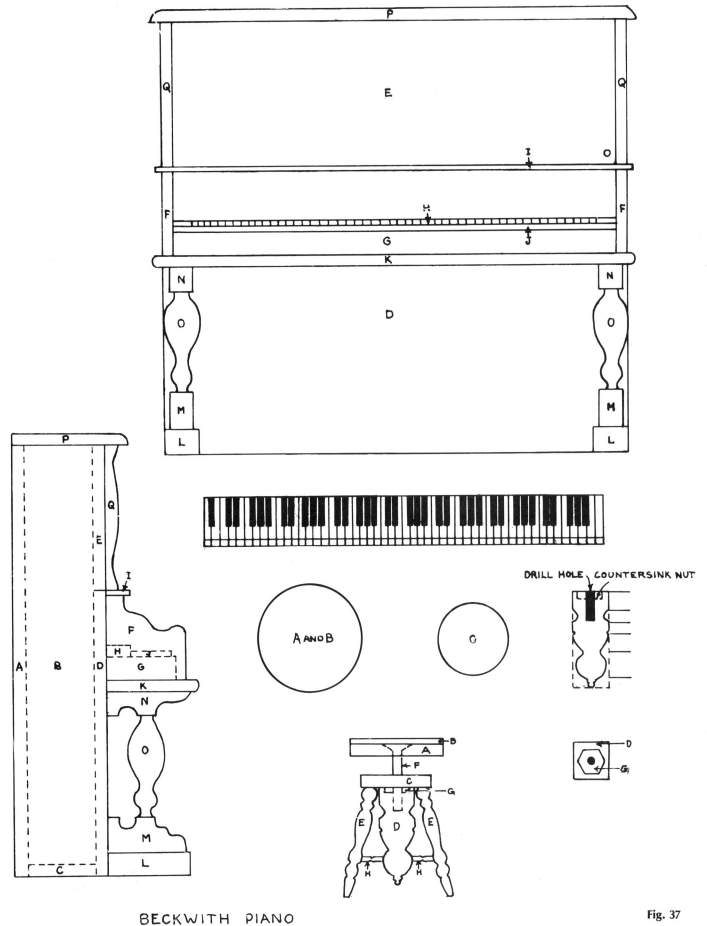

DRILL HOLE COUNTERSINK NUT

A AND B

G

BECKWITH PIANO

Fig. 37

MORRIS CHAIR, FIG. 38

1. Prepare the following for assembly. Identify all pieces by letter.

   A-1. Back frame, cut 2—2 1/2″ × 1/4″ × 1/8″
   A-2. Back frame, cut 2—1 1/4″ × 1/4″ × 1/8″
   B. Back slats, cut 4—2″ × 1/8″ × 1/16″
   C. Seat front—2″ × 3/8″ × 1/8″ (shaped)
   D. Seat sides, cut 2—2″ × 3/8″ × 1/8″
   E. Seat back—1 7/8″ × 3/8″ × 1/8″
   F. Seat slats, cut 4—2″ × 1/8″ × 1/16″
   G. Arms, cut 2—2″ × 3/8″ × 1/8″
   H. Spindles, cut 5—7/8″ × 3/32″ dowels
   I. Front legs, cut 2—1 7/8″ × 3/8″ × 1/8″
   J. Adjustment pins—10 sequin pins
   K. Adjustment bar—2 3/4″ wire
   L. Back legs, cut 2—1 7/8″ × 1/2″ × 1/8″

2. Glue seat front (C) between front legs (I).

3. Glue seat back (E) between back legs (L).

4. Glue seat sides (D) between front and back legs.

5. Glue and pin arms (G) to front and back legs. Glue spindles (H) between arms (G) and seat sides (D).

6. Glue reclining back frame together: A-2 top to A-1 sides, slats (B) to A-2 top, and then to A-2 bottom.

7. Hinge reclining back to back of seat (E). (See Furniture Construction, Hinges)

8. Space adjustment pins as shown and drive part way into the back edge of the back legs (L).

9. Sew two cushions to fit back and seat.

VICTROLA, FIG. 39

1. Prepare the following for assembly. Identify all pieces by letter.

   A. Back—2 5/8″ × 1 3/4″ × 1/8″
   B. Sides, cut 2—2 5/8″ × 7/8″ × 1/8″
   C. Base—2″ × 1 1/8″ × 1/8″
   D. Shelves, cut 4—1 1/2″ × 7/8″ × 1/16″
   E. Front—1 3/4″ × 1 3/8″ × 1/8″
   F. Molding, cut 2—1 1/4″ × 1/8″ × 1/16″
   G. Doors, cut 2—1 1/4″ × 3/4″ × 1/16″
   H. Front legs, cut 2—1/2″ × 1/2″ × 1/8″
   I. Back legs, cut 2—1/2″ × 1/4″ × 1/8″
   J. Turntable—5/8″ diameter × 1/32″ thick
   K. Turntable arm—handcarve of clay or wood
   L. Handle—1″ wire with 1/4″ handle (round)
   M. Lid top—1 5/8″ × 1″ × 1/16″
   N. Lid front and back, cut 2—1 3/4″ × 3/8″ × 1/8″
   O. Lid sides, cut 2—1″ × 3/8″ × 1/8″
   P. Lid trim, front and back—1 7/8″ × 1/16″ × 1/16″; sides, 1 1/8″ × 1/16″ × 1/16″

2. Cut hole in front panel (E) and glue tan-colored fabric in back. Glue a dark brown paper cutout to fabric in front.

3. Glue sides (B) between back (A) and front (E).

4. Glue unit to base (C) with back flush.

5. Hinge doors (G) to back of molding (F) with paper hinges.

6. Glue shelves (D) in cabinet.

7. Glue cabinet front with the hinged doors to sides (B).

8. Glue back legs (I) and front legs (H) to base (C).

9. Glue lid sides (O) between lid front and back (N).

10. Round corners of lid sides as shown.

11. Glue lid top (M) onto lid sides. Round edges.

12. Glue trim (P) around bottom edge of lid.

13. Hinge lid to back.

14. Drill hole in wood handle (L) and glue onto bent wire as shown.

15. Drill hole in right side (B) for wire handle. Bend end of wire on the inside to secure but so that it can still turn.

16. Glue turntable arm (K) and turntable (J) on shelf inside lid, as shown. Paint turntable top (J) bright green.

17. Paint victrola black.

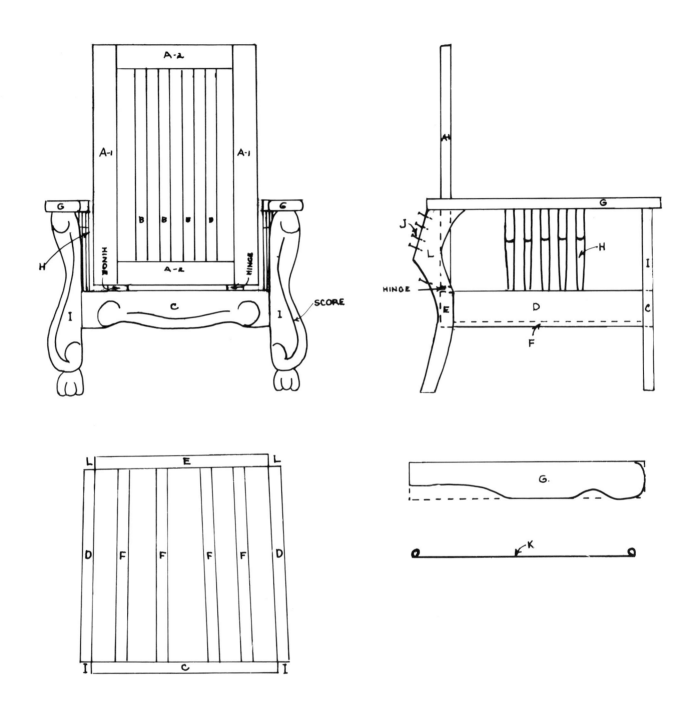

MORRIS CHAIR

Fig. 38

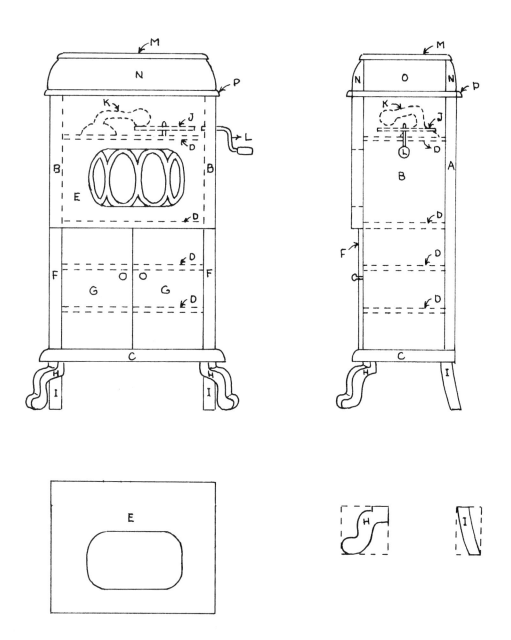

VICTROLA

Fig. 39

DINING ROOM

The dining room was used for evening meals and Sunday dinner, which was always 1:00 PM, after church at the Jellisons). The claw-footed, golden-oak pedestal table was placed in the center of the room on an oval needlepoint rug. The cherished Handel lamp may be seen on the table. This hand-painted lamp was a wedding present and is now quite valuable, being of the same vintage as the more famous but less rare Tiffany lamps. The large, round table is often seen in modern interiors cut down to cocktail table height.

A plate rail circles the room, displaying pewter plates and goblets, a silver box, brass dinner bell, plaque, and cups. The wall is painted as far up as the plate rail and wallpapered above with the same pattern used in the parlor.

The buffet, or sideboard, displays some of the family silver and crystal and stores the table linens. It also has a silverware drawer lined with felt. Our modern-day buffet, a stand-up, help-yourself service, is derived from the use of the buffet for holding side dishes, desserts, etc.

A curved front china cabinet, now a much sought-after collectible, displays the ironstone dinnerware, crystal dessert dishes, salt and pepper shakers, vinegar cruet, and serving dishes.

In the corner is the prized early Stewart Warner radio with its big horn. Too big for the parlor, the radio was placed adjacent to the parlor—within easy listening for the downstairs.

STEWART WARNER RADIO, FIG. 40

1. Prepare the following for assembly. Identify all pieces by letter.
   A. Top and base, cut 2—3/4" × 1 3/8" × 1/16"
   B. Front and back, cut 2—2 1/2" × 1" × 1/8"
   C. Sides, cut 2—1" × 7/8" × 1/8"
   D. Dial: cutout
   E. Knobs, cut 3—1/8" dowel slices

2. Glue sides (C) between front and back (B).

3. Glue unit centered to base (A).

4. Glue top (A) to tops of sides, front and back.

5. Glue knobs to front as shown.

6. Stain dark walnut.

7. Cut out dial (D) and glue to front. Varnish.

SPEAKER HORN, FIG. 40

1. Prepare the following for assembly. Identify all pieces by letter.
   A-1. Base: 7/8" diameter × 1/16"
   A-2. Base—5/8" diameter × 3/16"
   B. Curved neck—handcarve of wood
   C. Bell—tin

2. Glue base (A-2) to base (A-1).

3. Glue curved neck (B) to base (A-2).

4. Glue bell (C) to neck (B).

5. Paint black and glue to center of radio cabinet.

RADIO STAND, FIG. 40

1. Prepare the following for assembly. Identify all pieces by letter.
   A. Top—2 7/8" × 1 5/8" × 1/8"
   B-1. Apron, cut 2—2 5/8" × 1/4" × 1/16"
   B-2. Apron sides, cut 2—1 1/4" × 1/4" × 1/16"
   C. Legs, cut 4—2" × 1/8" square
   D. Shelf—2 5/16" × 1 1/16" × 1/16"

2. Glue apron front and back (B-1) to apron sides (B-2).

3. Glue top (A) to apron.

4. Glue and pin legs (C) into corners of apron.

5. Glue shelf (D) between legs.

6. Stain dark walnut and varnish.

PILLAR EXTENSION TABLE, FIG. 41

1. Prepare the following for assembly. Identify all pieces by letter.
   A. Top—3 3/4" diameter × 1/8"
   B. Legs, cut 4—2 3/8" × 1 1/4" × 3/8"
   C. Center pillar—7/8" diameter × 1 1/2"
   D. Apron—10 3/4" × 1/4" × 1/16"

2. Gouge design or score legs (B).

3. Glue center pillar (C) to exact center of top (A).

4. Bend apron (D) and glue to underside of top (A). (See Furniture Construction, Bending Wood)

5. Glue legs (B) to underside of table top (A) and to center pillar (C). Pin for extra strength.

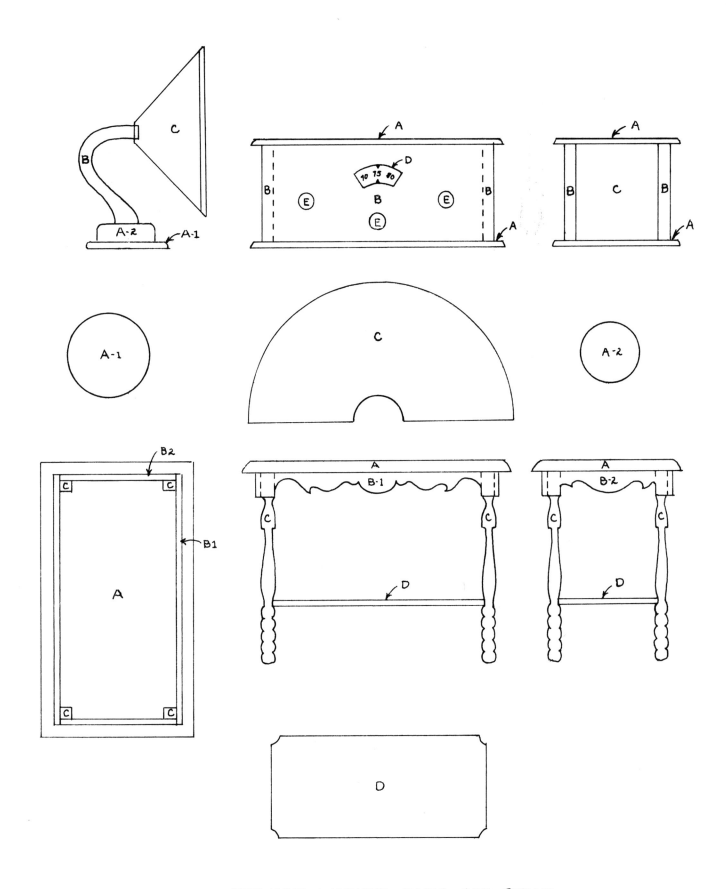

STEWART WARNER RADIO AND STAND

Fig. 40

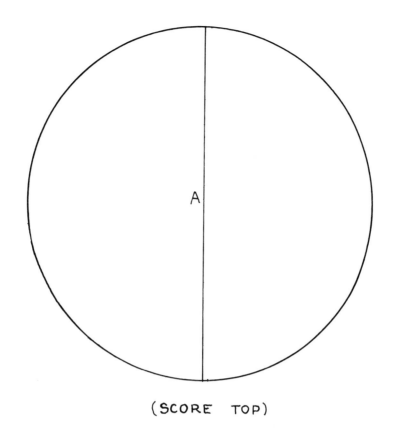

(SCORE TOP)

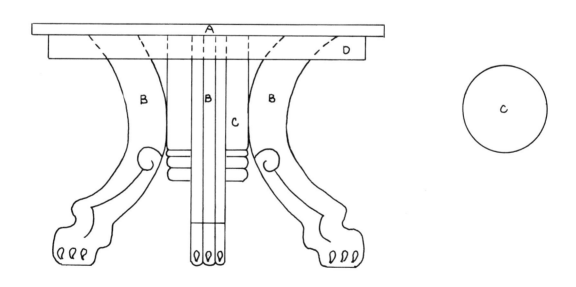

PILLAR EXTENSION TABLE

Fig. 41

CHINA CABINET, FIG. 42

1. Prepare the following for assembly. Identify all pieces by letter.
   A. Back—5" × 3 3/4" × 1/8"
   B. Top and bottom, cut 2—4" × 1 1/8" × 1/8"
   C. Shelves, cut 3—3 5/8" × 7/8" × 1/16"
   D-1. Side panel uprights, cut 2—3 1/2" × 1/8" × 1/16"
   D-2. Side panel top and bottom, cut 4—1 3/16" × 3/16" × 1/16"
   D-3. Side panel glass (acetate), cut 2—3 7/8" × 1 3/16"
   E-1. Front panel uprights, cut 4—3 1/2" × 3/16" × 1/16"
   E-2. Front panel top and bottom, cut 4—1 1/4" × 3/16" × 1/16"
   E-3. Front panel glass (acetate)—3 7/8" × 2 3/4"
   F. Feet, cut 4—5/8" × 5/8" × 3/8"
   G. Carved posts, cut 2—3 7/8" × 1/8" × 1/8"

2. Glue top and bottom (B) to back (A).

3. Glue feet (F) to bottom (B). Angle front feet from corner.

4. *Place carved posts (G) between top and bottom. Do not glue.*

5. Bend wood tops and bottoms (D-2, E-2) to fit just inside curve of top (B). (See Furniture Construction, Bending Wood)

6. Glue shelves (C) to back (A).

7. Glue side panels (D-1, D-2) to acetate (D-3), as shown.

8. Glue side panel units to back (A) and to top and bottom (B).

9. Glue carved posts (G) to side panels and top and bottom (B).

10. Glue front panels (E-1, E-2) to acetate (D-3), as shown. Make sure this unit will fit between carved posts (G).

11. Cut acetate with X-acto knife between front panels (E-1), to enable doors to open.

12. Hinge doors to back of carved posts (G).

13. Glue mirror (tin) in place above top (B) to back (A).

BUFFET SIDEBOARD, FIG. 43

1. Prepare the following for assembly. Identify all pieces by letter.
   A. Back—4 1/2" × 4" × 1/8"
   B. Sides, cut 2—4" × 1 1/2" ×1/8"
   C. Bottom—3 3/4" × 1 1/2" × 1/8"
   D. Center shelf—3 3/4" × 1 3/8" × 1/16"
   E. Drawer rest—3 3/4" × 1 1/2" × 1/16"
   F. Counter top—4 1/4" × 1 3/4" × 1/8"
   G. Top board—4 1/4" × 3/4" × 1/8"
   H. Front leg board—4 1/2" × 1/2" × 1/8"
   I. Center post—1 5/16" × 1/8" × 1/8"
   J. Drawer divider—3/8" × 1 1/2" × 1/8"
   K. Top board supports, cut 2—1 1/2" × 1/2" × 1/8"
   L. Counter shelves, cut 2—5/8" × 5/8" × 1/16"
   M. Front molding, cut 2—1 7/8" × 1/8" × 1/8"
   N. Drawer fronts, cut 2—1 13/16" × 3/8" × 1/8"
   O. Drawer bottoms, cut 2—1 13/16" × 1 3/8" × 1/16"
   P. Drawer backs, cut 2—1 13/16" × 1/4" × 1/16"
   Q. Drawer sides, cut 2—1 5/16" × 1/4" × 1/16"
   R. Door fronts, cut 2—1 13/16" × 1 7/16" × 1/8"

2. Glue bottom shelf (C) to back (A).

3. Glue center shelf (D) to back (A).

4. Glue drawer rest (E) to back (A).

5. Glue sides (B) to back (A).

6. Glue center post (I) to bottom shelf (C) and against underside of drawer rest (E).

7. Glue drawer divider (J) to top of drawer rest (E).

8. Glue counter top (F) to back (A), sides (B), and drawer divider (J).

9. Glue top board supports (K) to counter top (F).

10. Glue top board (G) to side supports (K) and back (A).

11. Glue counter shelves (L) to back (A) and against supports (K).

12. Glue front molding (M) to forward edges of sides (B).

13. Attach knobs and construct drawers (N, O, P, Q). (See Furniture Construction, Making a Drawer)

14. Attach knobs (sequin pins) and hinge doors (R). (See Furniture Construction, Hinges)

15. Glue tin mirror between counter shelves (L).

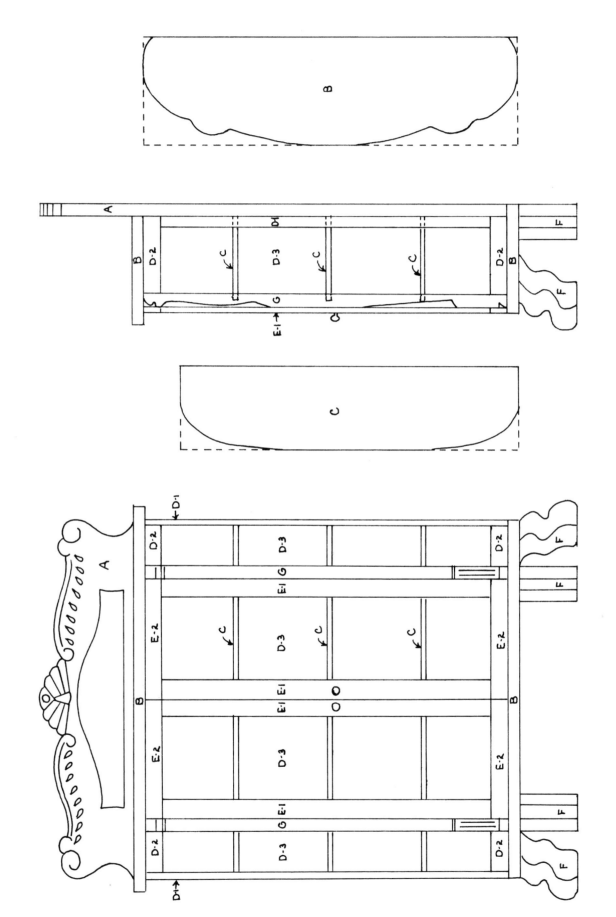

CHINA CABINET

Fig. 42

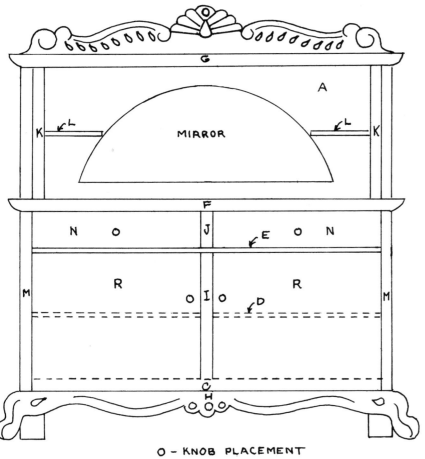
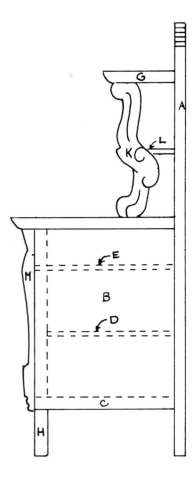

O – KNOB PLACEMENT

BUFFET SIDEBOARD

Fig. 43

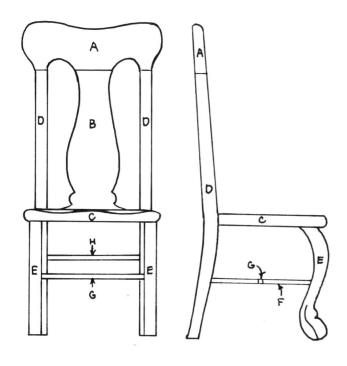

DINING ROOM CHAIR, FIG. 44

1. Prepare the following for assembly. Identify all pieces by letter.
   A. Top—1 1/2″ × 1/2″ × 1/8″
   B. Panel—1 9/16″ × 1″ × 1/16″
   C. Seat—1 1/2″ × 1 1/4″ × 1/8″
   D. Side backs, cut 2—1 3/4″ × 5/16″ × 1/8″
   E. Front legs, cut 2—1 3/16″ × 3/8″ × 1/8″
   F. Side rungs, cut 2—1 1/16″ × 1/16″ × 1/16″
   G. Front rung—1 1/8″ × 1/16″ × 1/16″
   H. Back rung—1″ × 1/16″ × 1/16″

2. Glue top of panel (B) to center of top (A).

3. Glue bottom of panel (B) to back of seat (C).

4. Pin and glue side backs (back legs) (D) to top (A) and the notch in seat (C).

5. Pin and glue front legs (E) 1/16″ from the underside of chair seat (C).

6. Glue side rungs (F) between front and back legs.

7. Glue front rung (G) between side rungs.

8. Glue back rung (H) between back legs.

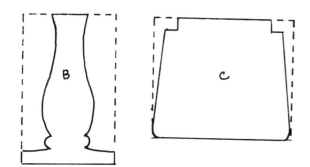

DINING ROOM CHAIR

Fig. 44

KITCHEN

Mother Jellison is in the kitchen, cooking at the stove, an early gas range on high legs with a side oven, which replaced the old, black, wood stove.

A dish of fruit is handy for snacks on the kitchen table, which has a drawer for cutlery. Four apple green chairs are used at the table for informal meals.

In the days before built-in cupboards the Hooiser kitchen cabinet was invaluable to the housewife, for this was the cooking center. It had a built-in flour-sifter (some styles had a sugar dispenser too), a bread drawer, two smaller drawers for cutlery, a pull-out cutting board, a large storage space below the worktop for pots and pans (with a door rack for spices and smaller lids), and cupboards above within easy reach for other cooking dishes or supplies. Glennie has just finished icing a cake, the eggs and a quart of milk still remain on the counter. The sliced bread on the cutting board is ready for the noon meal.

The gas refrigerator, commonly referred to as the "cake box," must have been a welcome addition to the kitchen of the 1920s. However, it was small, and many housewives kept their old ice boxes, if they had room, in a shed or back porch for additional cold storage.

The sink is white porcelain set in a wooden base and has a set-tub (deep-well) under the drain board. The set-tub was used for washing and rinsing clothes. After the electric washer was purchased, the machine was wheeled in from the shed and hooked up to the sink faucets every Monday morning (the traditional wash day). The used wash water was then drained into the set tub. The linoleum was always washed Monday morning after the laundry was done, since the floor got wet anyway.

The tie-back curtains with lace borders make the kitchen cheery and bright.

KITCHEN TABLE, FIG. 45

1. Prepare the following for assembly. Identify all pieces by letter.
   A. Top—4″ × 3″ × 1/8″
   B. Legs, cut 4—2 5/16″ × 1/4″ × 1/4″
   C. Front and back apron, cut 2—3″ × 1/2″ × 1/16″
   D. Side aprons, cut 2—2″ × 1/2″ × 1/16″
   E. Drawer front—1 1/2″ × 3/8″ × 1/16″
   F. Drawer runners, cut 2—2 1/4″ × 1/4″ × 1/16″

2. Glue apron (C, D) between legs (B), flush at top.

3. Glue and pin top (A) to apron and legs.

4. Construct drawer (See Furniture Construction, Making a Drawer)

5. Glue drawer runners (F) at the bottom edge of the apron, level with the bottom of the drawer.

GAS STOVE, FIG. 46

1. Prepare the following for assembly. Identify all pieces by letter.
   A-1. Back—4 3/4″ × 3 1/2″ × 1/8″ (cut out 2 1/4″ × 3″ bottom area to create 1/4″ straight legs)
   A-2. Front—2 3/4″ × 3 3/4″ × 1/8″ (cut out curved legs)
   B-1. Left oven side—2 1/4″ × 1 7/8″ × 1/8″
   B-2. Right oven side—1 3/4″ × 1 7/8″ × 1/8″
   C. Work top and bottom, cut 2—3 1/4″ × 1 7/8″ × 1/8″
   D. Stove side (right)—1/2″ × 1 7/8″ × 1/8″
   E. Oven top and bottom, cut 2—1 1/2″ × 1 7/8 × 1/8″
   F-1. Oven door—1 1/2″ × 1 1/2″ × 1/16″
   F-2. Oven door (inside)—1 3/8″ × 1 3/8″ × 1/8″
   G. Top shelf—1 3/4″ × 1/2″ × 1/16″
   H. Shelf support—1 11/16″ × 1/2″ × 1/16″
   I. Oven shelf—1 3/4″ × 1 1/2″ tin
   J. Gas burners, buy 4—1/2″ auto mechanics screws
   K. Gas controls—20-gauge wire, bent as shown.
   L. Oven handle—bent wire

2. Cut grooves 3/4″ up from bottom of oven sides (B-1, B-2) for placement of the tin oven shelf.

3. Glue oven side (B-1) to back (A-1).

4. Glue oven side (B-2) to back (A-1), 1 1/2″ to right of B-1.

5. Glue bottom (C) to back and oven side (B-1).

6. Cut holes in top (C) for placement of gas burners. Paint screws black and glue in holes.

7. Glue work top (C) against back (A-1), oven side (B-1), and to the bottom of oven side (B-2).

8. Glue right stove side (D) against back and between top and bottom (C).

9. Glue oven top and bottom (E) to oven sides (B-1, B-2).

10. Glue front legs (A-2) to oven side (B-1), right stove side (D), and work top and bottom (C). Round the front outside edges of legs and the edge of work top.

11. Glue oven door (F-2) to oven door (F-1).

12. Gently slide oven shelf (I) into grooves of oven sides.

13. Hinge oven door at bottom (E). (See Furniture Construction, Hinges)

14. Glue wire ends of gas controls (K) into 2 drilled holes in front (A-2).

15. Glue oven handle (L) into 2 drilled holes in oven door.

16. Cut out oven dial.

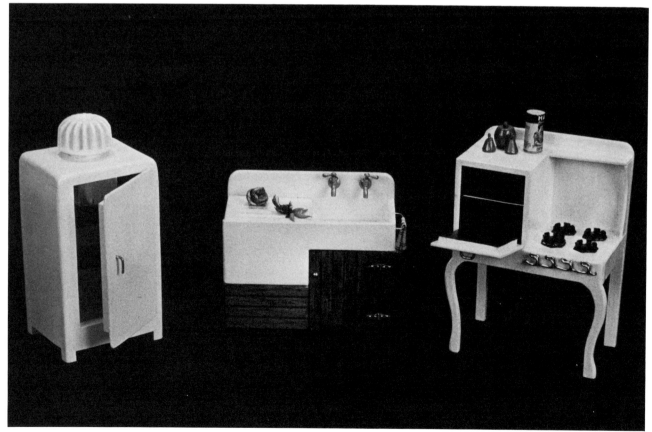

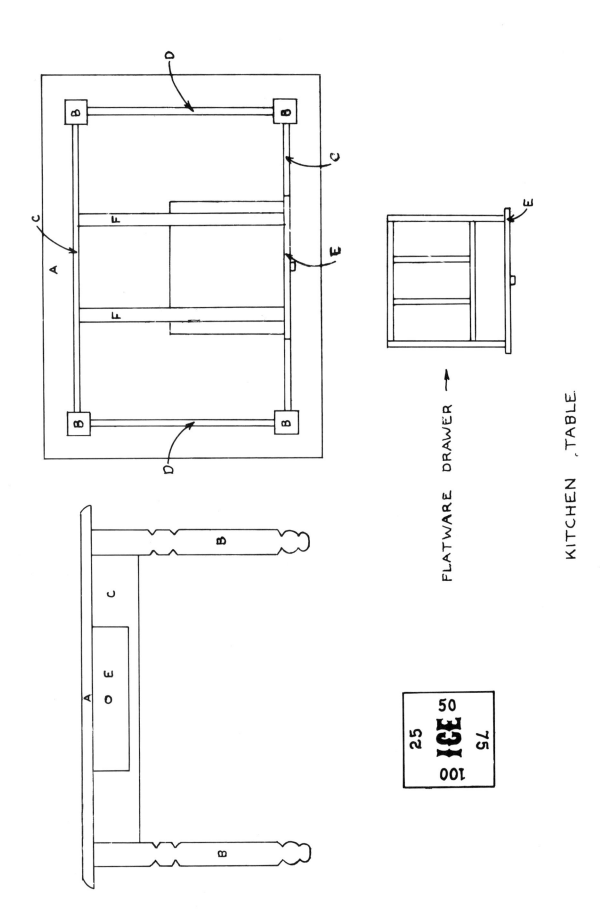

FLATWARE DRAWER

KITCHEN TABLE.

Fig. 45

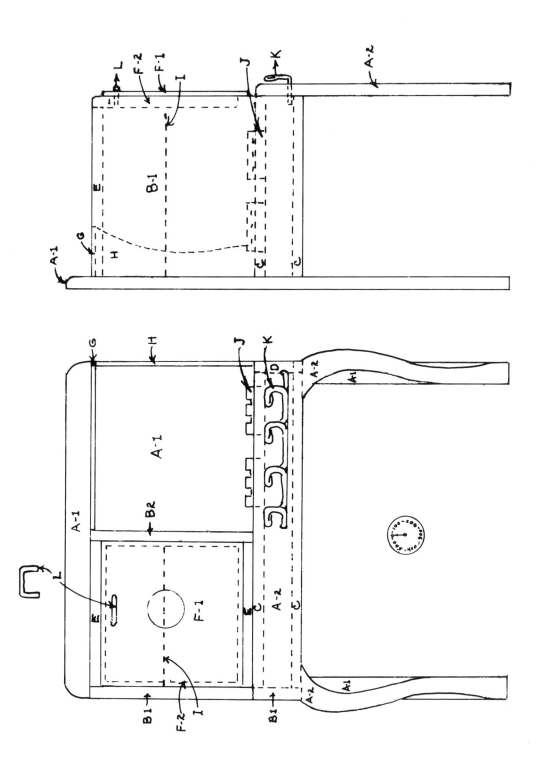

GAS STOVE

Fig. 46

17. Paint oven interior dark blue (may be speckled with white) and outside of stove white. Glue dial to oven front.

18. Spray with a clear, acrylic varnish until smooth and shiny.

KITCHEN SINK, FIG. 47

1. Prepare the following for assembly. Identify all pieces by letter.
  A. Back—4″ × 3 1/4″ × 1/8″
  B. Sides, cut 2—2 5/8″ × 1 1/2″ × 1/8″
  C. Middle upright—2 9/16″ × 1 1/2″ × 1/8″
  D. Tray—2 1/8″ × 1 1/2″ × 1/8″
  E. Sink bottom—1 7/8″ × 1 1/2″ × 1/8″
  F. Set-tub bottom—1 3/4″ × 1 1/2″ × 1/8″
  G. Sink front—4″ × 1 1/2″ × 1/8″
  H. Lower left front—1 3/4″ × 1 1/8″ × 1/8″
  I. Facing—2″ × 1/4″ × 1/8″
  J. Door—2″ × 1 3/4″ × 1/8″

2. Glue sides (B) to back (A).

3. Glue middle upright (C) to back (A).

4. Cut grooves in tray (D) as shown. Tray is removable.

5. Drill 1/4″ hole for drain in sink bottom (E) and glue to back (A), side (B), and middle upright (C). Set eyelet in hole.

6. Drill hole for drain in set-tub bottom (F) and glue to back, side, and middle. Set eyelet in hole.

7. Glue sink front (G) to sides and middle.

8. Round corners and paint sink white.

9. Score board effect into lower left front (H). Glue to side and middle.

10. Glue facing (I) to right side (B).

11. Score door (J) and hinge to right side facing (I).

12. Stain and varnish remaining wood.

13. Attach commercial dollhouse faucets to back (A).

CAKE BOX REFRIGERATOR, FIG. 48

1. Prepare the following for assembly. Identify all pieces by letter.
  A. Back—4″ × 2 1/2″ × 1/4″ (cut out 1/4″ legs)
  B. Sides, cut 2—3 3/4″ × 1 1/2″ × 1/4″
  C. Front—4″ × 2 1/2″ × 1/4″ (cut out 1/4″ legs at bottom and opening for door 3 1/4″ × 1 3/4″ starting at top)
  D. Shelves, cut 2—2 1/16″ × 1 1/4″ tin
  E. Ice compartment—tin
  F. Top—2 1/2″ × 2″ × 1/4″
  G. Bottom—1 1/2″ × 2″ × 1/4″
  H-1. Door—3 1/2″ × 2″ × 1/16″
  H-2. Door—3″ × 1 5/8″ × 1/4″
  I. Handle—20-gauge wire 5/8″ long
  J. Gas coils—plastic champagne cork

2. Cut grooves in sides (B) for shelves 1 1/2″ and 2 1/2″ from bottom.

3. Glue sides (B) to back (A) with grooves on inside. Paint the inside white.

4. Slide tin shelves (D) into grooves.

5. Cut and bend tin ice compartment (E). Glue flap.

6. Cut hole in top (F) to fit champagne cork. Paint underside of top white.

7. Glue ice compartment to underside of top, as shown.

8. Glue top (F) to back and sides with ice compartment inside box and cork on top.

9. Glue bottom (G) to back and sides.

10. Glue front (C) to sides and top.

11. Glue door (H-2) to the center of door (H-1).

12. Insert handle (I) into drilled hole.

13. Hinge door. (See Furniture Construction, Hinges)

14. Sand corners until nicely rounded.

15. Finish painting outside white. Spray with acrylic varnish until smooth and a high gloss is achieved.

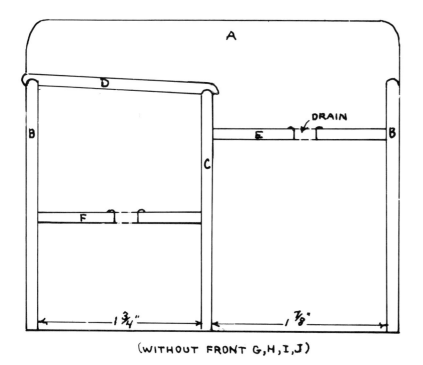

DRAIN

B   C   B

E

F

$1\frac{3}{4}''$ $1\frac{7}{8}''$

(WITHOUT FRONT G,H,I,J)

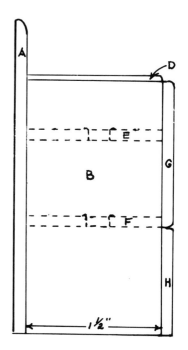

A

D

E

B   G

F

H

$1\frac{1}{2}''$

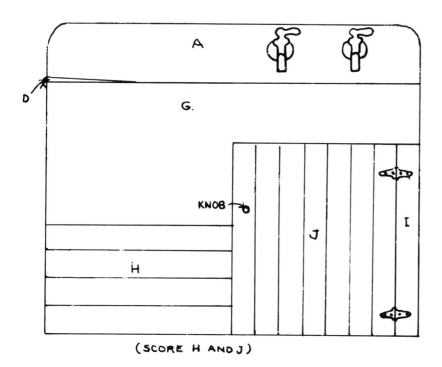

A

D

G.

KNOB

J   I

H

(SCORE H AND J)

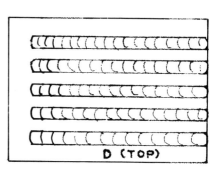

D (TOP)

KITCHEN SINK

Fig. 47

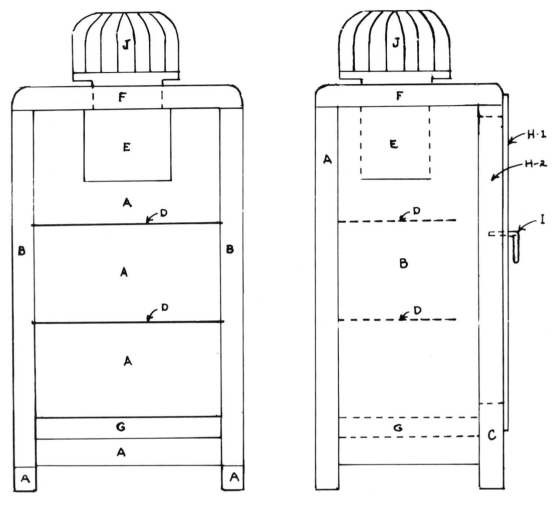

(WITHOUT FRONT C, H-1, H-2)

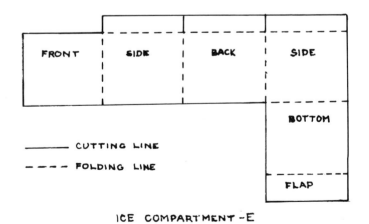

ICE COMPARTMENT-E

CAKE BOX REFRIGERATOR

Fig. 48

HOOSIER KITCHEN CABINET, FIGS. 49 AND 50

1. Prepare the following for assembly. Identify all pieces by letter.

Top:
   A. Back—3 3/4″ × 3 1/8″ × 1/8″
   B. Sides, cut 2—3 1/8″ × 1 1/8″ × 1/8″
   C. Top—4 1/2″ × 1 3/8″ × 1/8″
   D. Top decoration—4 1/2″ × 5/16″ × 1/8″
   E. Lower shelf—3 3/4″ × 1″ × 1/8″
   F. Upright dividers, cut 2—1 3/4″ × 1″ × 1/8″
   G. Side shelves, cut 3—1″ × 1″ × 1/16″
   H. Center shelves, cut 2—1 1/2″ × 1″ × 1/16″

Base:
   I. Back—3 3/4″ × 2 3/8″ × 1/8″
   J. Sides, cut 3 (one for middle divider)—2 3/4″ × 1 7/8″ × 1/8″
   K. Base—4 1/4″ × 2″ × 1/8″
   L. Front leg base—4 1/4″ × 5/16″ × 1/8″
   M. Drawer dividers, cut 3—1 1/2″ × 1 3/4″ × 1/16″
   N. Shelf—1 1/2″ × 2 1/8″ × 1/16″
   O. Side leg base, cut 2—3/4″ × 5/16″ × 1/8″
   P. Back leg base—4 1/4″ × 5/16″ × 1/8″
   Q. Counter top—4 1/2″ × 2 1/4″ × 1/8″

Fronts
   R. End doors, cut 2—1 1/8″ × 1 7/8″ × 1/8″
   S. Center door, frame sides—1 7/8″ × 3/16″ × 1/16″; top and bottom—1 1/4″ × 3/16″ × 1/16″; glass—1 3/4″ × 1 1/2″ acetate
   T. Bottom door—2 1/4″ × 2 3/8″ × 1/8″
   U. Drawer fronts, cut 2—1 5/8″ × 1/2″ × 1/8″
   V. Bread drawer front—1 5/8″ × 1 1/4″ × 1/8″
   W. Cutting board—1 3/4″ × 1 1/2″ × 1/8″
   X. Flour bin, round—2″ × 3/4″ tin (see diagram); top—4 1/4″ × 1 1/4″ (square); bottom—3 1/4″ × 5/8″
   Y. Door rack, sides—1 3/4″ × 5/8″ × 1/16″ (cut 2); top shelf—1 3/8″ × 7/16″ × 1/16″; bottom shelf—1 3/8″ × 5/8″ × 1/16″; bars—1 3/8″ × 1/8″ × 1/16″
   Z. Bread drawer, top—1 1/2″ × 7/8″ × 1/16″ (cut 2); sides—1 3/4″ × 1″ × 1/16″; back—1 3/8″ × 1″ × 1/16″; bottom—1 11/16″ × 1 3/8″ × 1/16″

2. Top directions: Glue sides (B) to back (A).

3. Glue top decoration (D) to back of top (C).

4. Glue top to sides and back.

5. Glue upright dividers (F) one inch from each side and against top.

6. Drill holes in left center of lower shelf (E) and center of left shelf (G) 3/8″ in diameter.

7. Glue lower shelf (E) against back (A) and sides (B).

8. Glue shelves (G, H) against back and sides as shown.

9. Base Directions: Glue sides and middle divider (J) to back (I).

10. Glue sides and back to base (K).

11. Glue shelf (N) and drawer dividers (M) against back and sides as shown.

12. Glue counter top (Q) to sides and back.

13. Glue side leg bases (O) between front leg base (L) and back leg base (P).

14. Glue base unit to base legs.

15. Glue top unit to counter top (Q).

16. Front Directions: Bevel outside edges of end doors (R), bottom door (T), drawer fronts (U), and bread drawer front (V).

17. Glue center door (S) sides, top, and bottom frames to acetate "glass," as shown.

18. Attach knobs and hinge doors (See Furniture Construction, Hinges)

19. Construct drawers (U) and attach knobs (See Furniture Construction, Making a Drawer)

20. Construct bread drawer (sides against bottom), hinge top, and attach knobs (wood dowels or pin heads).

21. Attach knob to front edge of cutting board (W).

22. Bend tin parts for flour (see diagram). Glue as shown into left side of cabinet. Attach 1/4″ wire handle.

23. Stain and varnish.

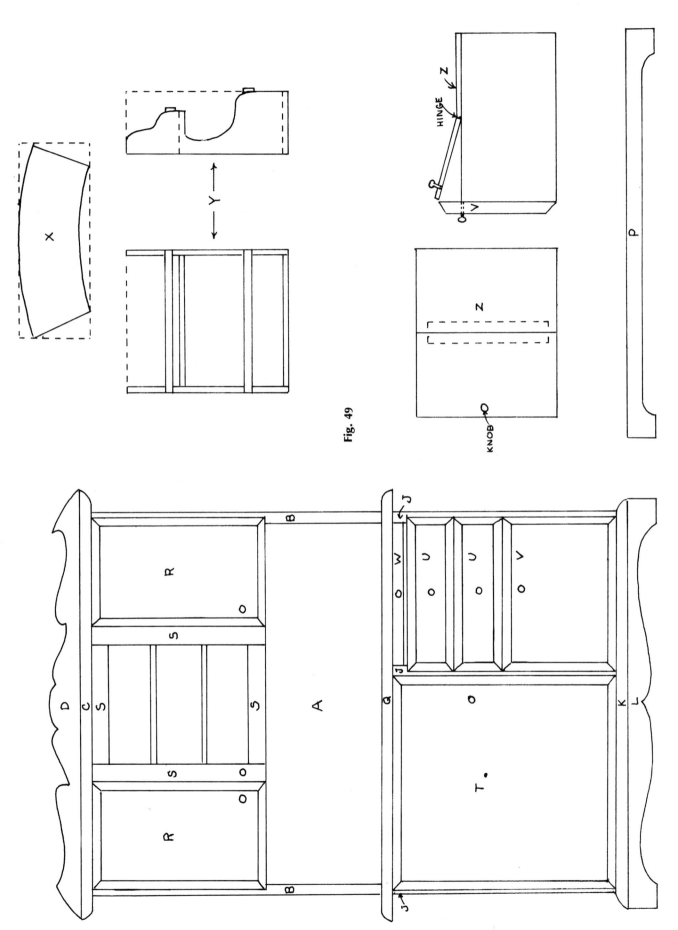

Fig. 49

HOOSIER KITCHEN CABINET

84

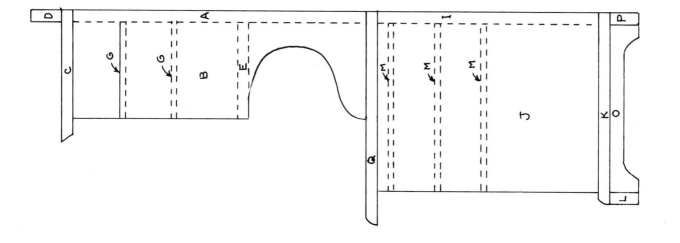

Fig. 50

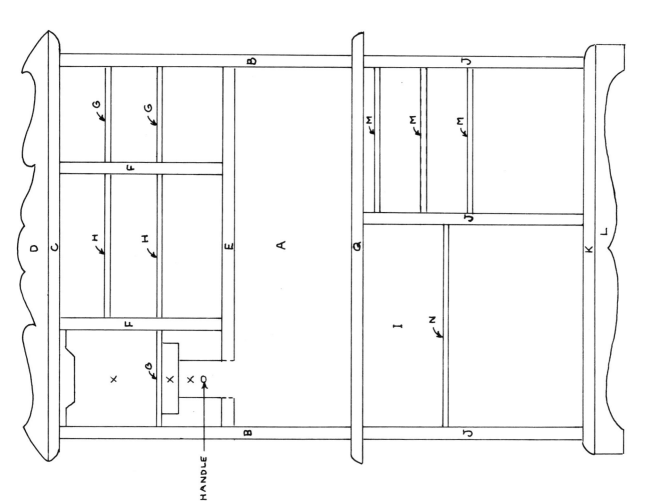

HOOSIER KITCHEN CABINET

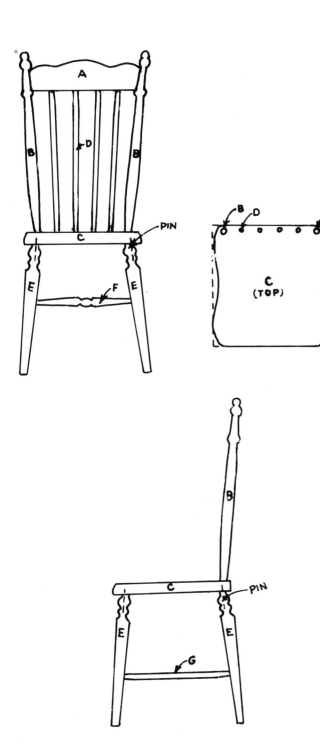

KITCHEN CHAIR

Fig. 51

KITCHEN CHAIR, FIG. 51

1. Prepare the following for assembly. Identify all pieces by letter.
   A. Back—1 3/16″ × 5/16″ × 1/16″
   B. Side posts, cut 2—1 7/8″ × 1/8″ dowel
   C. Seat—1 1/4″ × 1 1/4″ × 1/8″
   D. Spindles, cut 4—1 1/2″ + 1/16″ dowel
   E. Legs, cut 4—1 3/8″ × 1/8″ dowel
   F. Front and back rungs, cut 2—1″ × 1/16″ dowel
   G. Side rungs, cut 2—1 1/8″ × 1/16″ dowel

2. Drill slight indentations in seat (C) for side posts (B).

3. Glue back (A) between side posts (B).

4. Glue spindles (D) to back (A).

5. Glue side posts (B) and spindles (D) to seat (C).

6. Glue and pin legs (E) to bottom of seat (C).

7. Glue front and back rungs (F) to legs (E).

8. Glue side rungs (G) to legs (E).

SHED

Here we find the old ice box, still handy and in use for extra cold storage. Notice the tongs that hang above it. There was a hole drilled in the floor under the ice chest for water drainage. The shed's built-in shelves hold old newspapers, crocks, jugs, mortar and pestle, funnels, basket (with cabbage from the garden), a bushel of potatoes, and a variety of canned goods. The cellar was generally used for home-preserved food, including Mother Jellison's delicious root beer, which used to explode occasionally while fermenting. For the long winter months a coal furnace provided heat through a network of pipes in the cellar leading to floor registers.

A flyswatter hangs on the shed wall, along with an old black pot and ladle. A braided rug is just inside the door for wiping feet before entering the main house.

On the laundry side of the shed, the copper clothes boiler, stirring fork, and wash board are kept, along with cleaning items such as the mop, scrub brush, broom, rug beater, and carpet sweeper (the forerunner of our electric broom and vacuum cleaner). (The electric washing machine came later.) The ironing board and iron are in a state of readiness (it must be Tuesday), and there are tea towels and Charlie's overalls drying on the line.

A rag rug is on the floor and a shovel in the corner. Brown and white curtains "adorn" the window. There was seldom a curtainless window in 1920s houses.

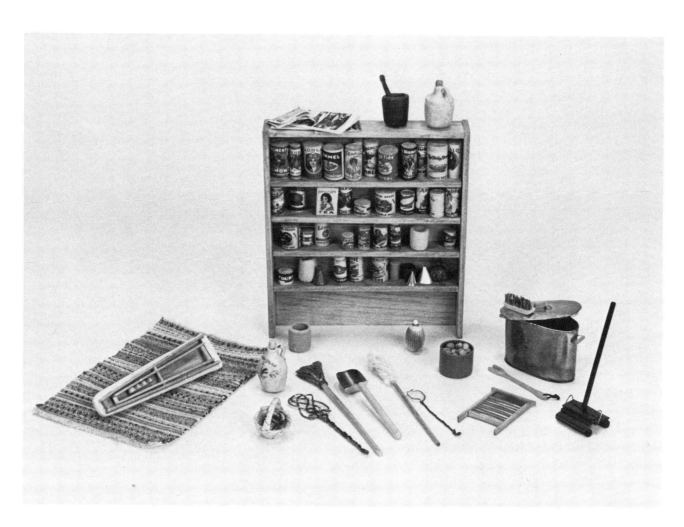

ICE CHEST, FIG. 52

1. Prepare the following for assembly. Identify all pieces by letter.
   A. Back—4 1/4" × 2 1/4" × 1/4" (cut 1/4" legs)
   B. Sides, cut 2—4" × 1 3/4" × 1/4"
   C. Front top—2 1/4" × 1 1/2" × 1/4"
   D. Front bottom—2 1/4" × 1/2" × 1/4" (cut 1/4" legs)
   E. Lift top—2" × 1" × 1/4"
   F. Ice compartment bottom and chest bottom, cut 2— 2 1/4" × 1 1/4" × 1/8"
   G. Door—2" × 2" × 1/4"
   H. Shelf—1 1/4" × 2 1/4" tin

Outside Trim:
   I. Sides, cut 4—4 1/4" × 5/16" × 1/16"
   J. Sides, cut 8—1 1/8" × 5/16" × 1/16"
   K. Front (verticals) cut 2—4 1/4" × 3/8" × 1/16"
   L. Front (horizontals) cut 3—2 1/8" × 3/8" × 1/16"
   M. Lift top, cut 2—2 1/2" × 5/16" × 1/16"
   N. Lift top, cut 2—3/4" × 5/16" × 1/16"
   O. Door (verticals) cut 2—2 5/16" × 3/8" × 1/16"
   P. Door (horizontals) cut 2—1 9/16" × 3/8" × 1/16"
   Q. Top, cut 2—2 15/16" × 3/8" × 1/16"
   R. Top, cut 2—1 1/16" × 3/8" × 1/16"

2. Glue sides (B) to back (A) with sides covering edges of back. (Back will be *between* sides and flush at top.)

3. Glue front pieces (C, D) *between* sides at top and bottom, flush at top, cut-out feet at bottom.

4. Line the inside of the box with tin or tin foil brought all the way to front edge and top openings. Use Quik glue.

5. Indent a groove at shelf lines (H) and slide shelf into grooves.

6. Cover one side of top (E) with tin.

7. Cover one side of door (G) with tin.

8. Glue top trim (M, N) onto edge of top (E), which will fit into hole with the trim extension to act as a lip. Tin inside.

9. Glue door trim (O, P) to edge of door (G), which will fit into hole with the trim extension to act as a lip. Tin inside door.

10. Glue top trim (Q, R) around hole.

11. Glue sides trim (I, J) and front trim (K, L) to outside of box, as shown.

12. Attach dollhouse hinges and handles.

SHED SHELVES, FIG. 53

1. Prepare the following for assembly. Identify all pieces by letter.
   A. Shelves, cut 5—4 1/4" × 3/4" × 1/8"
   B. Sides, cut 2—6" × 3/4" × 1/8"

2. Glue and pin shelves (A) between sides (B), as shown.

IRONING BOARD, FIG. 54

1. Prepare the following for assembly. Identify all pieces by letter.
   A. Top—3 3/4" × 1" × 1/8" (taper one end to 1/2")
   B. Wide legs, cut 2—3 5/8" × 1/8" × 1/16"
   C. Wide brace—3/4" × 1/8" × 1/8"
   D. Brace—5/16" × 1/16" × 1/16"
   E. Narrow legs, cut 2—3 1/8" × 1/8" × 1/16"
   F. Narrow brace—1/2" × 1/16" × 1/16"
   G. Brace—3/16" × 1/16" × 1/16"
   H. Adjusting cleat—3/4" × 1/8" × 1/8"
   I. Center dowel—9/16" × 1/16" × 1/16" (toothpick)

2. Cover top (A) with white cotton fabric. Glue 1/8" to underside of board.

3. Glue wide brace (C) between wide legs (B) at one end.

4. Glue brace (D) between wide legs (B) at the other end.

5. Drill 1/16" holes in narrow legs (E) for center dowel (I).

6. Glue narrow brace (F) between narrow legs (E) at one end.

7. Glue brace (G) between narrow legs (E) at the other end.

8. Glue adjusting cleat (H) to underside of top (A) as shown.

9. Cut paper hinge 11/16" × 3/8". Glue hinge to wide brace (C) and onto large end of top (A).

10. Glue ends of dowel (I) to inside of wide legs (B) with dowel inserted through holes in narrow legs (E). (Holes may have to be enlarged slightly for easy movement.)

IRON, FIG. 54

1. Prepare the following for assembly. Identify all pieces by letter.
   A. Base—7/16" × 5/16" × 1/8"
   B. Handle—5/16" × 3/32" dowel
   C. Wire—1 1/4"

2. Drill hole lengthwise through handle (B) for wire (C).

3. Insert wire (C) through handle with equal amounts at both ends.

4. Drill holes in base (A), as shown. Bend wire to fit into holes.

5. Glue ends of wire and insert into holes.

6. Paint base black and stain handle.

7. Instructions for making the carpet sweeper, mop, broom, etc. are given in the Accessories chapter.

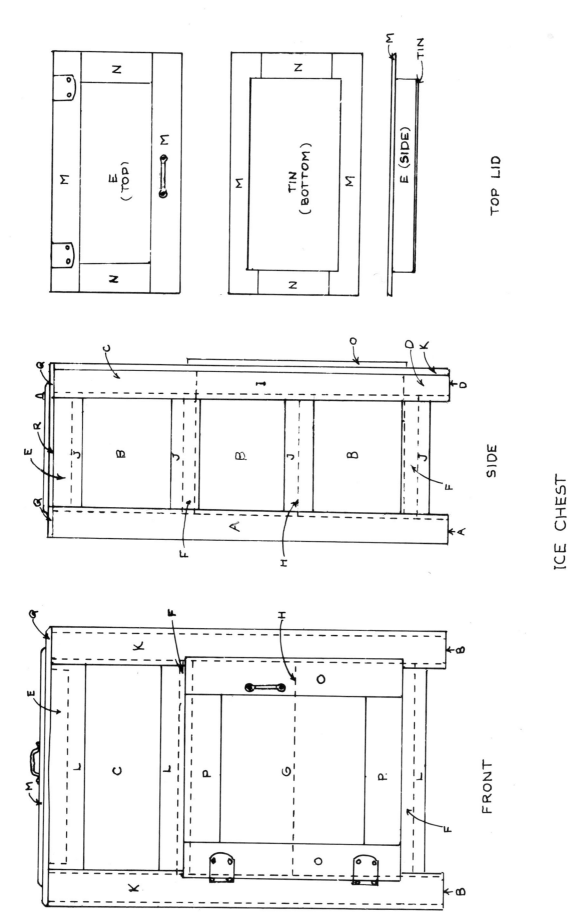

TOP LID

SIDE

FRONT

ICE CHEST

Fig. 52

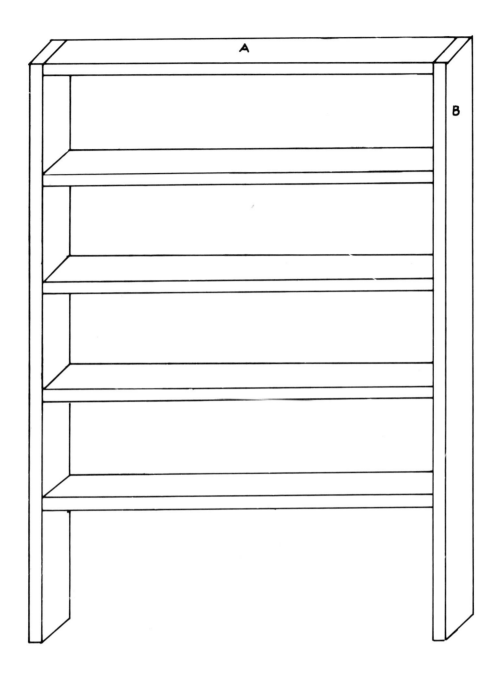

SHED SHELVES

Fig. 53

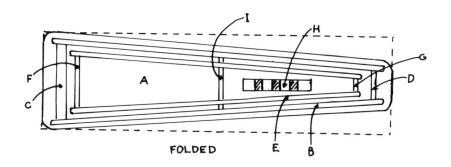

FOLDED

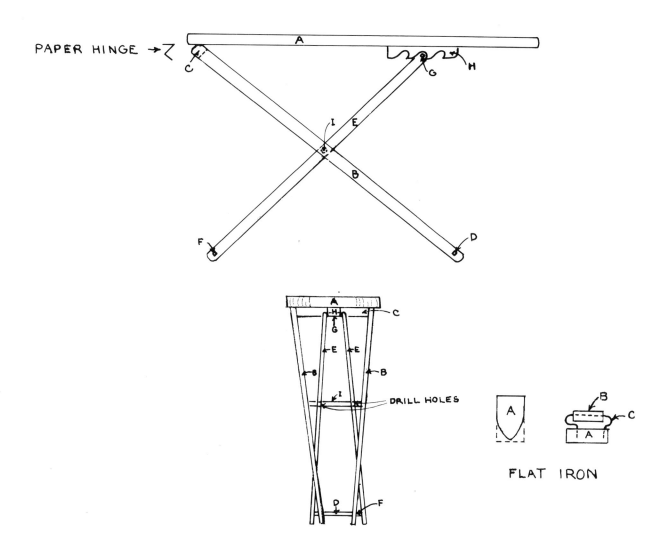

PAPER HINGE →

DRILL HOLES

FLAT IRON

IRONING BOARD

Fig. 54

PORCH

A welcome mat invites visitors to enter at the front door. The adjustable sun curtains, or shades, on the side porch help to keep the porch cool and private. There is a checkered-pattern sisal rug under the porch swing.

Charlie's favorite summer spot was on the swing which was also handy for "spooning." There he is in his knickers, taking life easy while dreaming of one day being miraculously "discovered" by the Boston Red Socks.

The red geraniums on the metal flower stand and the yellow tulips on the window sill add a touch of color and interest. Flowers were usually found on porches in those days. Flags were also common. I'm still looking for a small American flag to hang out in front of the house, one with forty-eight stars.

PORCH SWING, FIG. 55

1. Prepare the following for assembly. Identify all pieces by letter.
   A. Back, cut 2—4 1/2" × 1/8" × 1/16"
   B. Sides, cut 2—1 11/16" × 1/8" × 1/8"
   C-1. Seat back—4 1/2" × 1/4" × 1/8"
   C-2. Seat front—4 3/4" × 1/4" × 1/8"
   D. Back slats, cut 14—1 1/16" × 3/16" × 1/16"
   E. Arm rests, cut 2—1 5/8" × 1/4" × 1/8"
   F. Seat ends, cut 2—1 5/16" × 1/8" × 1/8"
   G. Seat slats, cut 4—4 3/4" × 3/16" × 1/8"
   H. Arm supports, cut 2—5/8" × 1/8" × 1/8"
   I. Chain—2 feet of jewelry chain
   J. Hooks—6 sequin pins

2. Glue backs (A) to slats (D) in flat position.

3. Bevel ends of sides (B) and glue slat unit between sides.

4. Glue seat back (C-1) between sides (B).

5. Bevel one end of arm rests (E) and seat ends (F).

6. Glue arm rests (E) and seat ends (F) to sides (B).

7. Glue arm supports (H) to arm rests (E) and seat ends (F).

8. Glue seat front (C-2) to seat ends (F) and arm supports (H).

9. Glue seat slats (G) to top of seat ends (F).

10. Clip heads off sequin pins and bend into U shape. Drill holes in arm rests and ceiling. Glue ends of pins and slip chain link through pin before insertion into wood.

GERANIUM, FIG. 55

1. Prepare the following for assembly. Identify all pieces by letter.
   A. Pot—wood or clay, 1/2" top
   B. Flower—clay or paper
   C. Stem—florist wire
   D. Leaf—clay or paper

2. Shape pot and fill with soft florist clay.

3. Shape flowers from long strips of thin air dry clay wound around and pinched together. Flatten small balls for the leaves.

4. Paint pot and soil. Paint flowers and leaves.

5. Insert florist wire stems into clay and glue flowers and leaves onto stems.

TULIPS, FIG. 55

1. Prepare the following for assembly. Identify all pieces by letter.
   A. Pot—wood or clay, 3/8" top
   B. Flowers—clay or paper
   C. Stem—florist wire
   D. Leaves—clay or paper

2. Shape pot and fill with clay.

3. Cut points into long strip of thin clay. Wind around in a circle and smooth the bottoms. Cut leaf shapes from thin rolled-out clay.

4. Paint pot and soil. Paint flowers and leaves.

5. Insert florist wire stems into clay soil and glue flowers and leaves onto stems.

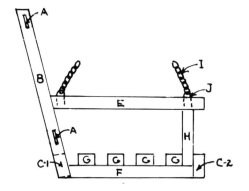

METAL STAND, FIG. 55

1. Prepare the following for assembly. Identify all pieces by letter.
   E. Top—1/2″-diameter tin
   F. Stem—3/32″ wood dowel
   G. Base—1 1/8″-diameter tin

2. Pin top (E) to stem (F).

3. Bend base (G) and pin to stem (F).

4. Paint black.

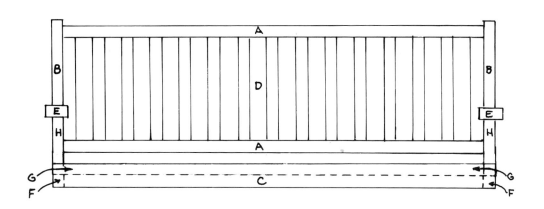

PORCH SWING

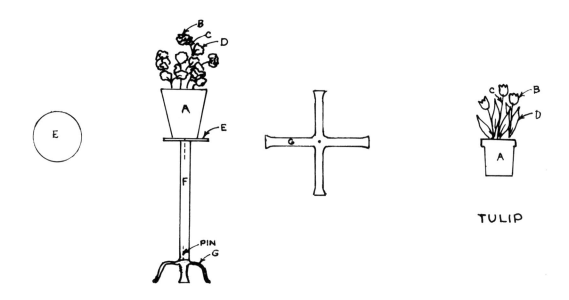

GERANIUM AND STAND

TULIP

Fig. 55

MASTER BEDROOM AND HALL

The "golden-oak" suite (Sears and Roebuck, 1928) was the pride and joy of Mother and Dad Jellison. Not so ornate as earlier Victorian pieces, it still had a lot of rococo decoration.

The bedside table holds a lamp, cold cream jar, and photograph case. There are matching lamps on the dresser, along with crystal perfume bottles and two gold powder and hair containers. Ladies of the 1920s had given up saving their hair for "rats," but the containers were still useful for pins, buttons, etc.

In the corner there is a wing chair with a matching foot stool, upholstered in a brown and yellow flowered fabric. The striped scatter rugs go with the handsome striped wallpaper.

The picture on the wall, which can't be seen in the photograph, is a Godey Ladies print, fashionably framed in gold. Just outside the master bedroom in the hall hangs a familiar Currier and Ives print in a mahogany frame. At the foot of the attic steps there is an embroidered sampler that reads: "A Friendship True is like pure gold—It won't wear out because it's old."

All the curtains in the front of the house are made of lace, in the fashion of the times. I remember my own mother spending hours stretching newly washed lace curtains over frames with protruding nails so that they would dry to window size without ironing. Of course, the nails always pulled little scallops into the edges that no amount of ironing could erase.

BED, FIGS. 56 AND 57

1. Prepare the following for assembly. Identify all pieces by letter.
   Headboard:
   A. Top—5 1/2" × 1/2" × 1/8"
   A-2. Top rest—5" × 3/8" × 1/8"
   B. Posts, cut 2—4 3/4" × 1/4" × 1/4" (square)
   C. Back—4 1/4" × 3 1/2" × 1/8"
   D. Molding, cut 2—4 1/4" × 1/8" dowel
   E. Molding, cut 2—4 1/4" × 1/2" × 1/16"
   F. Molding, cut 2—4" × 1/2" × 1/16"
   G. Molding, cut 2—4 1/4" × 5/16" × 1/16"
   Footboard:
   H. Top—5" × 3/8" × 1/8"
   I. Posts, cut 2—3" × 1/4" × 1/4" (square)
   J. Back—4 1/4" × 1 3/4" × 1/8"
   K. Side rails, cut 2—6" × 1" × 1/8"
   L. Brace, cut 2—6" × 1/8" × 1/8"
   M. Slats, cut 9—4 1/4" × 1/4" × 1/16"

2. Glue headboard top (A) to forward edge of top rest (A-2).

3. Glue posts (B) to ends of back (C), with back flush.

4. Glue molding (D, E, F, G) to back, as shown.

5. Glue footboard posts (I) to back (J).

6. Glue footboard top (H) *centerd* to posts and back.

7. Glue molding (D, E, F, G) to back, as shown.

8. Glue and pin footboard and headboard together with bed side rails (K).

9. Glue braces (L) to inside bottom edge of side rails (K), which will support slats.

10. Glue slats (M) across bed to support springs and mattress.

DRESSER, FIG. 58

1. Prepare the following for assembly. Identify all pieces by letter.
   A-1. Top—4" × 3/8" × 1/8"
   A-2. Top rest—3 3/4" × 3/8" × 1/8"
   B. Posts, cut 2—3 3/8" × 3/16" × 3/16" (square)
   C. Mirror Base—2 7/8" × 2 7/8" × 1/8"
   D. Mirror molding, cut 4—5/8" × 5/8" × 1/16"
   E. Mirror brace—3" × 5/16" × 1/8"
   F. Mirror shelf—3" × 3/16" × 1/16"
   G. Mirror—2 5/8"-diameter tin
   H. Chest top—3 3/4" × 1 7/8" × 1/8"
   I. Chest back—3" × 2 1/2" × 1/8"
   J. Chest sides, cut 2—2 1/2" × 1 1/4" × 1/8"
   K. Chest legs (posts), cut 4—2 5/8" × 1/4" × 1/4"
   L. Drawer fronts, cut 3—3" × 5/8" × 1/8"
   M. Chest facing—3" × 3/8" × 1/8"
   N. Side paneling, cut 4—1 1/4" × 1/2" × 1/16"
   O. Side paneling, cut 2—1 1/2" × 1/4" × 1/16"
   P-1. Drawer rest—3" × 1 5/8" × 1/8"
   P-2. Drawer rests, cut 2—3" × 1 9/16" × 1/8"

2. Glue top (A-1) to top rest (A-2) 1/16" back from the forward edge.

3. Glue mirror brace (E) between posts (B) with bottoms and back flush.

4. Glue top unit to tops of posts (B) with back flush.

5. Glue mirror shelf (F) to top of mirror brace (E), as shown.

6. Glue mirror molding (D) to corners of mirror base (C).

7. Glue mirror (G) to mirror base (C).

8. Drill holes and insert pins into the side of mirror unit and into the side of posts.

9. Glue chest sides (J) between chest legs (K) with uncarved posts at rear and inside and top flush.

10. Glue chest back (I) between side units with outside and top flush.

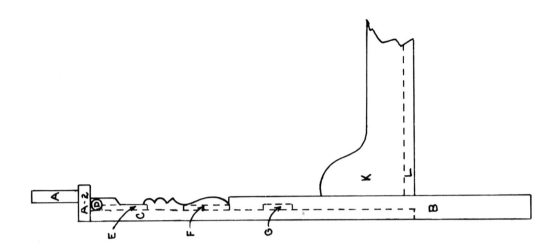

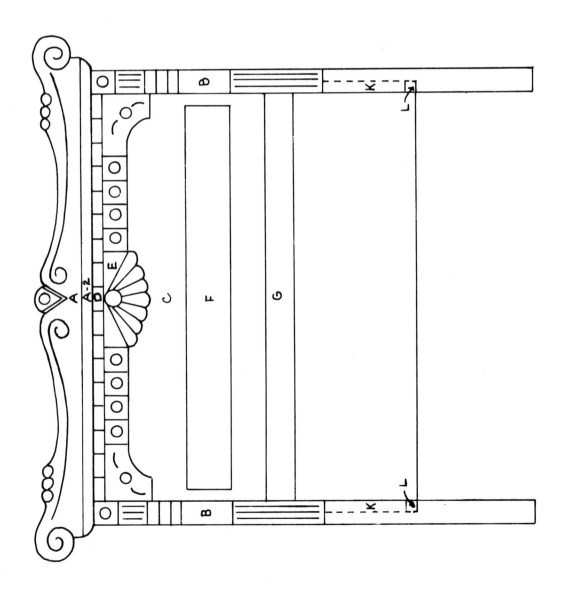

BED HEADBOARD

Fig. 56

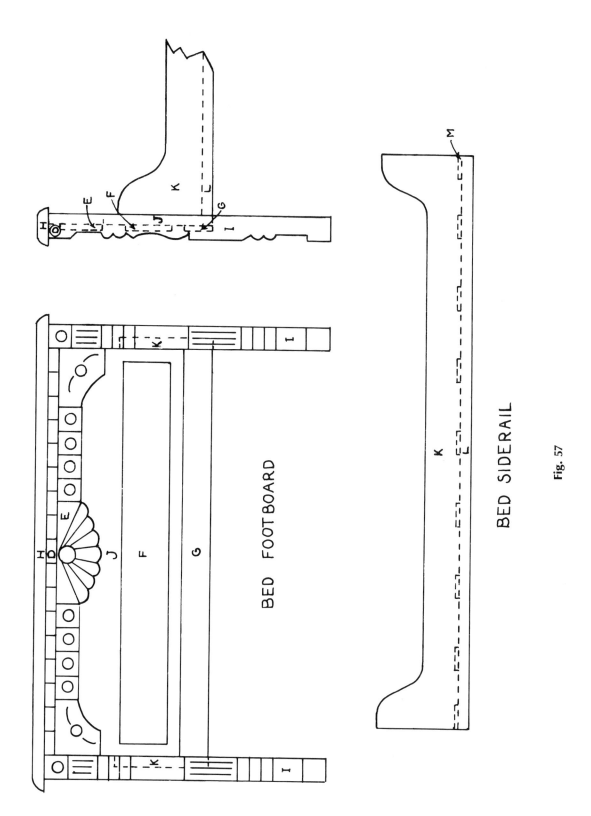

BED FOOTBOARD

BED SIDERAIL

Fig. 57

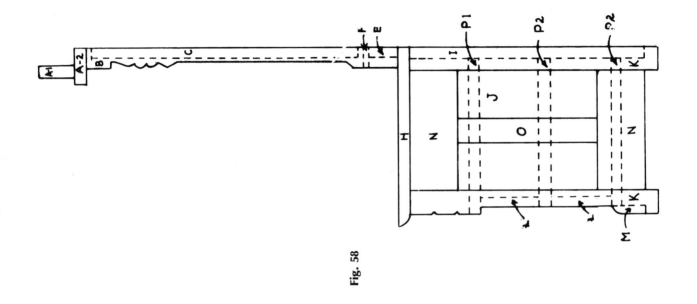

Fig. 58

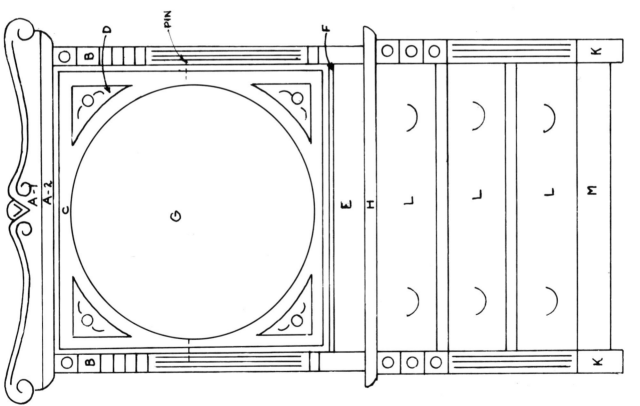

DRESSER

11. Glue drawer rests (P-1, P-2) to back and sides of chest with P-1 at top. (Measure drawer space of 5/8″ accurately.)

12. Glue chest facing (M) to front between carved legs and to lower drawer rest.

13. Glue top (H) to chest unit.

14. Glue side paneling (N, O) to sides (J) as shown.

15. Construct drawers (L). (See Furniture Construction, Making a Drawer)

16. Glue and pin mirror unit to chest unit.

WASHSTAND, FIG. 59
1. Prepare the following for assembly. Identify all pieces by letter.
    A. Upper back—2 3/4″ × 5/8″ × 1/8″
    B. Back—2 1/4″ × 2 3/8″ × 1/8″
    C. Top—2 7/8″ × 1 1/2″ × 1/8″
    D. Posts, cut 4—2 1/2″ × 3/16″ × 3/16″
    E. Facing—2 1/4″ × 7/16″ × 1/8″
    F. Upright divider—1 1/2″ × 1 1/16″ × 1/8″
    G. Drawer divider—1″ × 1 1/16″ × 1/8″
    H. Drawer rest and lower shelf, cut 2—2 1/4″ × 1 1/8″ × 1/16″
    I. Side drawer fronts, cut 2—1″ × 11/16″ × 1/16″
    J. Top drawer front—2 1/4″ × 3/8″ × 1/16″
    K. Door front—1 1/2″ × 1 1/8″ × 1/16″
    L-1. Door-molding verticals, cut 2—1/12″ × 3/16″ × 1/16″
    L-2. Door-molding horizontals, cut 2—3/4″ × 3/16″ × 1/16″
    L-3. Door-molding center—1″ × 1/2″ × 1/16″
    M. Top side pieces, cut 2—3/8″ × 3/8″ × 1/16″
    N. Sides, cut 2—2 3/8″ × 7/8″ × 1/8″
    O-1. Side-molding horizontals, cut 4—7/8″ × 1/2″ × 1/16″
    O-2. Side-molding verticals, cut 2—1 3/8″ × 3/16″ × 1/16″

2. Glue washstand sides (N) between posts (D) with uncarved posts at rear and inside and top flush.

3. Glue washstand back (B) between side units with outside and top flush.

4. Glue drawer rest (H) and lower shelf (H) to back and sides of chest.

5. Glue upright divider (F) and drawer divider (G) to back and sides of chest.

6. Glue facing (E) to front between carved posts (D) and to lower shelf (H).

7. Glue top (C) to chest unit.

8. Glue upper back (A) to rear of top in upright position.

9. Glue top side pieces (M) to top and back 1/4″ from side edges.

10. Construct drawers (I, J). (See Furniture Construction, Making a Drawer).

11. Glue door moldings (L-1, L-2, L-3) to door (K), as shown.

12. Hinge door. (See Furniture Construction, Hinges)

BEDSIDE TABLE, FIG. 60
1. Prepare the following for assembly. Identify all pieces by letter.
    A. Top—1 3/4″ × 1 3/4″ × 3/32″
    B. Legs, cut 4—2″ × 3/8″ × 1/8″
    C. Shelf—1 1/8″ × 1 1/8″ × 1/16″

2. Glue and pin legs (B) to top (A). Angle legs outward.

3. Glue shelf (C) to inside of legs (B).

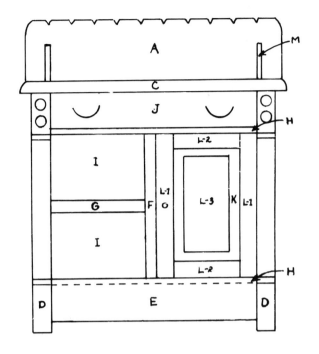
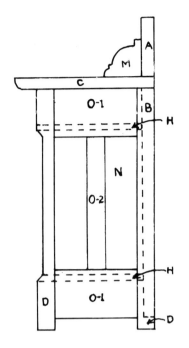

WASHSTAND

Fig. 59

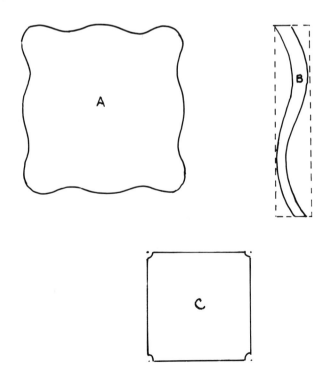
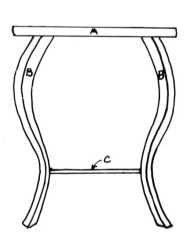

BEDSIDE TABLE

Fig. 60

CHARLIE'S BEDROOM

Charlie's bedroom sports a handsome brass bed covered with a homespun bedspread. The bed was formerly used in the master bedroom until the new "golden-oak" suite replaced it. The tall chiffonier with adjustable mirror—similar in style to the earlier Colonial highboy—is a practical chest of drawers.

The table by the bed, originally a "parlor table," was eventually destined to be painted and used as a flower stand on the porch.

A very practical and popular piece of furniture at this time was the oak desk-bookcase combination. The desk front dropped forward and rested on the drawer underneath to create a writing surface. The pigeon holes in the desk held a collection of baseball trading cards as well as pencils, paper, etc. The books were kept on the shelves to the left of the desk. A dining-room style chair served as a desk chair.

The wallpaper is a blue-and-white "Victorian" design suitable for a boy's room. The old miniature map of the United States hanging on the wall was replaced some years later by Betty Grable and Gloria DeHaven pinups.

BRASS BED, FIG. 61

The brass bed, or any reproduction made with beads, is pretty much dependent on what beads you have available. The technique used is variable as well. I used a combination of beads (from an old necklace) and wooden dowels for the main post construction. The wooden dowels secure the beads and stengthen the frames. A good grade of gold paint (See Suppliers) will make the dowels look almost as metalic as the beads. For a uniform finish you may paint the beads with gold paint as well.

1. Prepare the following for assembly. Identify all pieces by letter.
   A. Cut 2—2 15/16″ × 3/16″ dowel
   B. Cut 4—15/16″ × 3/16″ dowel
   C. Cut 4—4″ × 1/8″ dowel
   D. Cut 2—3″ × 3/32″ dowel
   E. Cut 2—2 1/2″ × 3/32″ dowel
   F. Cut 2—1 5/16″ × 3/32″ dowel
   G. Cut 2—1 15/16″ × 1/8″ dowel

2. Paint wooden dowels gold.

3. Pin beads into wood (A, B), as shown.

4. Drill holes for jewelry pins in C and E. Measure carefully on a straight line drawn on the dowels and do not drill all the way through where the point of the pin is inserted.

5. Glue around pin head shaft and insert pin point through bottom of C, string beads, glue point, and insert into E.

6. Glue around pin head shaft and insert pin point through E, string beads, glue point, and insert into top C.

7. Pin and glue D to top and bottom C, then into E. Dry in flat position.

8. Pin and glue ends of C into posts A and B.

9. Repeat steps 2 through 8 for foot of bed.

10. Construct springs (See Fig. 62)

11. Pin and glue springs at top of B (below middle bead).

2. Glue braces to springs and bed posts.

BED SPRINGS, FIG. 62

1. Prepare the following for assembly. Identify all pieces by letter.
   A. Side rails, cut 2—6″ × 1/8″ × 1/16″
   B. End rails, cut 2—4 1/4″ × 1/8″ × 1/16″
   C. Wire—72″ florist wire
   C-1. Wire, for 28 ties, each 3/4″ long
   D. Braces, cut 4—3/4″ × 3/32″ × 1/16″

2. Drill holes for wire in side and end rails (A, B), as shown.

3. String wire (C) loosely through holes. Fasten ends securely.

4. Pull wire (C) together with ties (C-1), twist in middle, and clip ends underneath.

5. Glue and pin springs to bed and reinforce braces (D) glued to springs and bed posts.

PARLOR TABLE, FIG. 63

1. Prepare the following for assembly. Identify all pieces by letter.
   A. Top—1 3/4″ × 1 3/4″ × 3/32″
   B. Legs, cut 4—2″ × 3/8″ × 1/8″
   C. Shelf—1 1/4″ × 1 1/4″ × 1/16″

2. Glue and pin legs (B) to top (A), angled outward.

3. Glue shelf (C) to inside of legs (B).

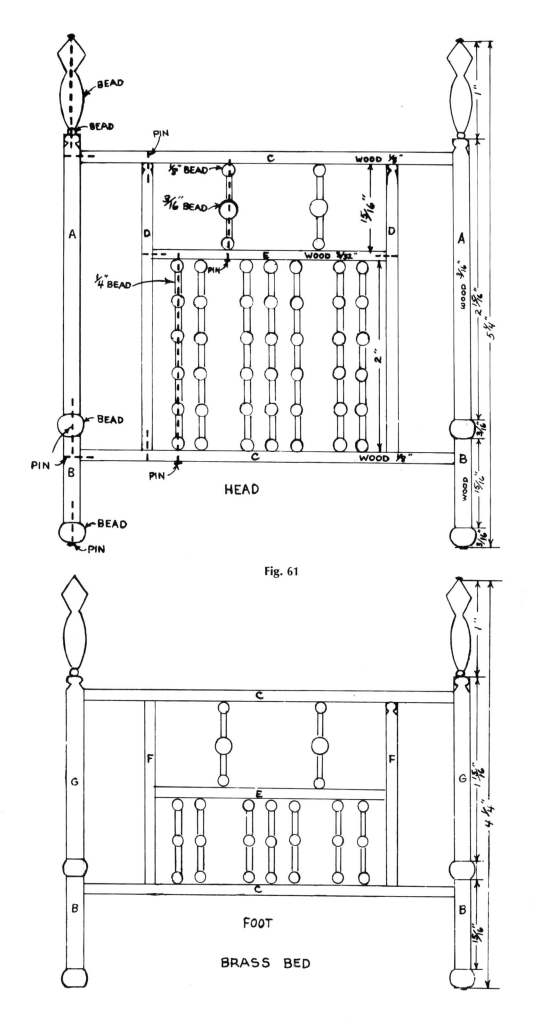

BEAD

BEAD

PIN

C

WOOD 1/8"

1/8" BEAD

3/16" BEAD

A

D

D

15/16"

WOOD 3/16"

2 1/8"

5 1/4"

A

E

WOOD 3/32"

1/4" BEAD

PIN

2"

BEAD

3/16"

PIN

B

C

WOOD 1/8"

B

15/16"

WOOD

PIN

PIN

3/16"

HEAD

Fig. 61

C

F

F

G

1 1/16"

G

E

4 1/4"

B

C

B

15/16"

FOOT

BRASS BED

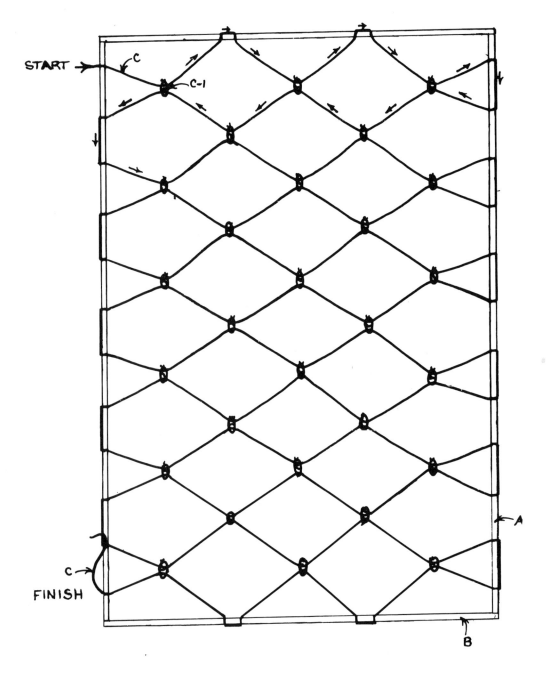

BED SPRINGS

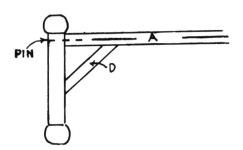

Fig. 62

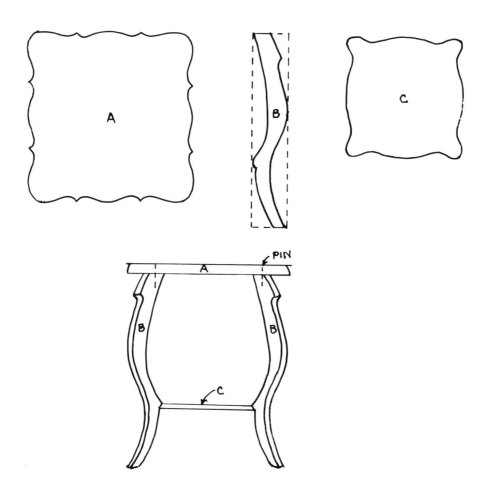

PARLOR TABLE

Fig. 63

CHIFFONIER, FIG. 64

1. Prepare the following for assembly. Identify all pieces by letter.
   A. Back—3 3/4″ × 2 1/8″ × 3/32″
   B. Sides, cut 2—3 3/4″ × 1 1/8″ × 3/32″
   C. Shelves, cut 6—2 1/8″ × 1 3/8″ × 1/16″
   D. Bottom apron—2 1/8″ × 1/4″ × 1/16″
   E. Top—2 3/4″ × 1 5/8″ × 3/32″
   F. Legs, cut 4—4″ × 3/16″ × 3/16″
   G. Side trim, cut 4—1 1/8″ × 1/4″ × 1/16″
   H. Top drawer front—2 1/8″ × 5/8″ × 3/32″
   I. Lower drawer fronts, cut 4—2 1/8″ × 11/16″ × 3/32″
   J. Drawer pulls—dollhouse hardware
   K. Mirror support—2 3/4″ × 1 1/4″ × 3/32″
   L. Mirror frame—1 7/8″ × 1 1/2″ × 3/32″
   M. Mirror—cut tin slightly smaller than frame

2. Glue chest sides (B) between legs (F), with outside and top flush.

3. Glue chest back (A) between side units (B), with outside and top flush.

4. Glue shelves (C) for drawer rests at intervals shown. Top drawer is not as deep as the others.

5. Glue top (E) to sides (B), back (A), and top shelf (C).

6. Glue bottom apron (D) under last shelf (C) and between front legs.

7. Construct drawers (H, I). (See Furniture Construction, Making a Drawer)

8. Attach drawer pulls (J).

9. Glue mirror (M) to back of frame (L).

10. Pin mirror frame (L) to mirror support (K), as shown.

11. Glue unit to top (E) at back edge.

DESK-BOOKCASE, FIG. 65

1. Prepare the following for assembly. Identify all pieces by letter.
   A. Back—6″ × 3″ × 1/16″
   B. Left side—5 1/4″ × 1 7/16″ × 1/16″
   C. Right side—4 1/4″ × 1 7/16″ × 1/16″
   D. Middle upright—4 11/16″ × 1 7/16″ × 1/16″
   E. Desktop: 1 11/16″ × 1/12″ × 1/16″
   F. Shelves, cut 3—1 1/8″ × 1 5/16″ × 1/16″
   G. Writing surface and drawer rest, cut 2—1 11/16″ × 1 7/16″ × 1/16″
   H. Bottom—2 7/8″ × 1 7/16″ × 1/16″
   I. Bookcase top—1 7/16″ × 1 1/8″ × 1/16″
   J. Desk upright—1 7/16″ × 1 1/2″ × 1/16″ (cut at same angle as C)
   K. Pigeon hole sides—1 1/16″ × 7/16″ × 1/16″
   L. Pigeon hole bottom—1 1/4″ × 7/16″ × 1/16″
   M. Pigeon hole division—1 1/8″ × 7/16″ × 1/16″
   N. Pigeon hole division, cut 2—3/4″ × 7/16″ × 1/16″
   O. Handles—sequin pin heads
   P. Base front—3 3/16″ × 1/2″ × 1/16″
   Q. Door frame top and bottom, cut 2—1 1/8″ × 1/8″ × 1/16″ (beveled)
   R. Door frame sides, cut 2—4 1/2″ × 1/8″ × 1/16″ (beveled)
   S. Drawer front—1 11/16″ × 3/8″ × 1/16″
   T. Door front—1 11/16″ × 1 3/8″ × 1/16″
   U. Mirror—1 1/4″ × 1″ tin
   V. Desk front—1 3/4″ × 1 1/16″ × 1/16″

2. Glue left side (B) to back (A), flush at bottom.

3. Glue right side (C) to back (A).

4. Glue bottom (H) between left side (B) and right side (C) and to back (A).

5. Glue middle upright (D) to bottom (H) and back (A) allowing exactly 1 1/8″ space for bookcase and 1 11/16″ for desk.

6. Glue bookcase top (I) between left side (B) and middle upright (D), as shown.

7. Glue shelves (F) between left side (B) and middle upright (D).

8. Glue desk top (E) and drawer rest and writing surface (G) between middle upright (D) and right side (C).

9. Glue desk upright (J), cut at same angle as right side (C), between desk top (E) and writing surface (G).

10. Glue pigeon holes (K, L, M, N) together, as shown. Glue to back (A).

11. Glue base front (P) to left side (B) and right side (C).

12. Glue door frames (Q, R) to acetate 4 1/2″ × 1 1/8″ (glass).

13. Attach door to right side with paper hinges. (See Furniture Construction, Hinges)

14. Construct drawer (S). (See Furniture Construction, Making a Drawer)

15. Glue mirror (U) to back (A).

16. Attach desk front (V) to writing surface (G) with paper hinges.

17. Attach front door (T) to right side (C) with paper hinges.

DESK CHAIR (SEE DINING ROOM CHAIR, FIG. 44)

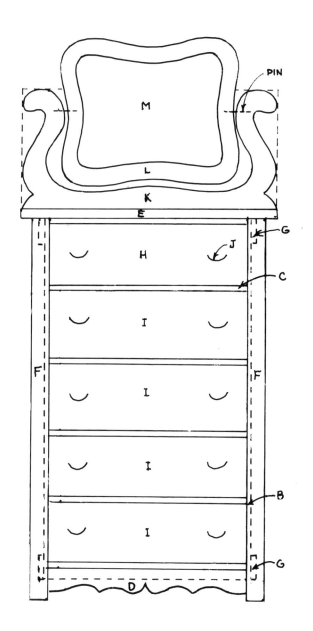

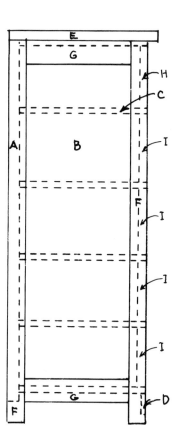

CHIFFONIER

Fig. 64

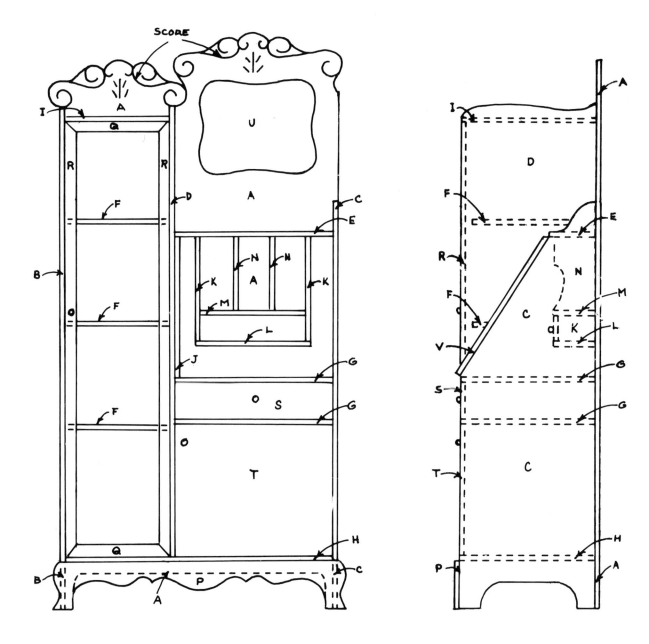

DESK - BOOKCASE

Fig. 65

POLLY'S BEDROOM

The pink wallpaper with little red bows seems just right for a girl's bedroom.

Polly's walnut slat bed and walnut dresser with adjustable mirror are small in size but are in proportion to the small room she occupies. The lady's desk, made of golden oak, has a drop front that rests on the pulled-out drawer underneath. Polly is a serious student, as the Webster's dictionary and Atlas on the desk attest. The desk chair has turned legs and spindles. This type was sometimes called the occasional chair, which means, I think, that it could be used anywhere.

The cameo hanging on the wall is set in an ornate frame. The wall lamp was once lighted by gas. A hand-woven red-and-white rug and pink linen curtains with open-work borders complete the decor.

OCCASIONAL CHAIR, FIG. 66

1. Prepare the following for assembly. Identify all pieces by letter.
    A. Seat—1 5/16″ × 1 5/16″ × 1/8″
    B. Back—1″ × 1/4″ × 1/16″
    C. Side posts, cut 2—1 7/8″ × 3/16″ dowel
    D. Spindles, cut 4—1 3/8″ × 3/32″ dowel
    E. Legs, cut 4—1 7/16″ × 3/16″ dowel
    F. Front and back rungs, cut 2—1 1/4″ × 1/16″ dowel
    G. Side rungs, cut 2—1 1/8″ × 1/16″ dowel

2. Drill slight indentations in seat (A) for side posts (C) and spindles (D).

3. Glue back (B) between side posts (C).

4. Glue spindles (D) to back (B).

5. Glue side posts (C) and spindles (D) to seat (A).

6. Glue and pin legs (E) to bottom of seat (A).

7. Glue front and back rungs (F) to legs (E).

8. Glue side rungs (G) to legs (E).

LADY'S DESK, FIG. 67

1. Prepare the following for assembly. Identify all pieces by letter.
    A. Back—2 1/4″ × 1 3/4″ × 1/8″
    B. Sides, cut 2—3 1/4″ × 1 1/8″ × 1/8″
    C. Top—2 5/8″ × 3/4″ × 1/16″
    D. Back board—2 5/8″ × 1/2″ × 1/16″
    E. Desk surface and drawer rest, cut 2—2 1/4″ × 1/8″ × 1/16″
    F. Drawer front—2 1/4″ × 5/16″ × 1/16″
    G. Desk front—2 5/8″ × 1 5/16″ × 1/16″
    H. Pigeon holes, cut 4—5/8″ × 1/2″ × 1/32″
    I. Pigeon holes—2 1/4″ × 1/2″ × 1/32″
    J. Pigeon holes—1 1/8″ × 1/2″ × 1/32″
    K. Pigeon holes—5/16″ × 1/2″ × 1/32″
    L. Drawer front—1 1/8″ × 5/16″ × 1/32″
    M. Mirror—1 3/4″ × 5/16″ tin

2. Glue sides (B) to back (A).

3. Glue desk surface and drawer rest (E) to sides (B) and back (A).

4. Glue pigeon holes (H, I, J, K) against sides (B) and back (A).

5. Glue top (C) to tops of pigeon holes and sides.

6. Glue back board (D) to rear of top (C).

7. Glue mirror (M) to back board (D).

8. Construct drawers (F, L). (See Furniture Construction, Making a Drawer)

9. Attach hardware.

WALNUT BED, FIG. 68

1. Prepare the following for assembly. Identify all pieces by letter.
    Headboard:
    A. Back—3″ × 3″ × 1/8″
    B. Posts, cut 2—4″ × 1/4″ × 1/4″
    C. Top molding—3″ × 1/2″ × 1/16″
    D. Middle molding—3″ × 1/4″ × 1/16″
    E. Lower molding—3″ × 3/8″ × 1/16″
    Footboard:
    F. Back—3″ × 2″ × 1/8″
    G. Top—3 3/4″ × 3/8″ × 1/8″
    H. Posts, cut 2—3″ × 1/4″ × 1/4″
    I. Top molding—3″ × 1/4″ × 1/16″
    J. Lower molding—3″ × 3/8″ × 1/16″
    Sides:
    K. Rails, cut 2—5 3/4″ × 5/8″ × 1/8″
    L. Braces, cut 2—5 3/4″ × 1/8″ × 1/8″
    M. Slats, cut 8—3 1/4″ × 1/4″ × 1/16″

2. Glue headboard posts (B) to ends of back (A) with back flush.

3. Glue moldings (C, D, E) to back (A).

4. Glue footboard posts (H) to back (F).

5. Glue top (C) to posts and back.

6. Glue moldings (I, J) to back (F).

7. Glue and pin footboard and headboard together with bed siderails (K).

8. Glue braces (L) to inside bottom edge of siderails (K).

9. Glue slats (M) across bed to support springs and mattress.

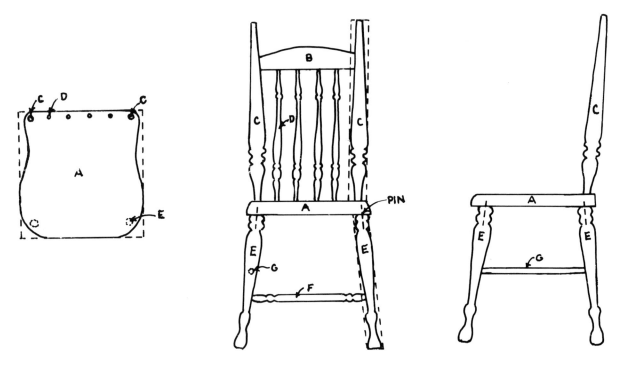

OCCASIONAL CHAIR

Fig. 66

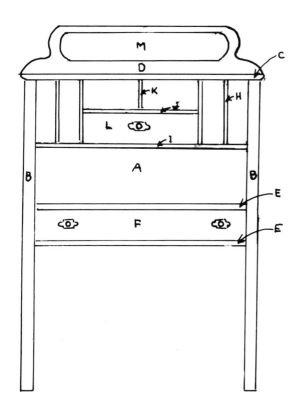

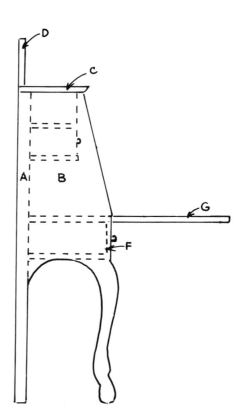

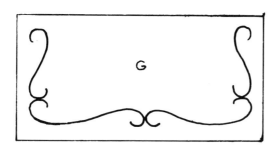

LADY'S DESK

Fig. 67

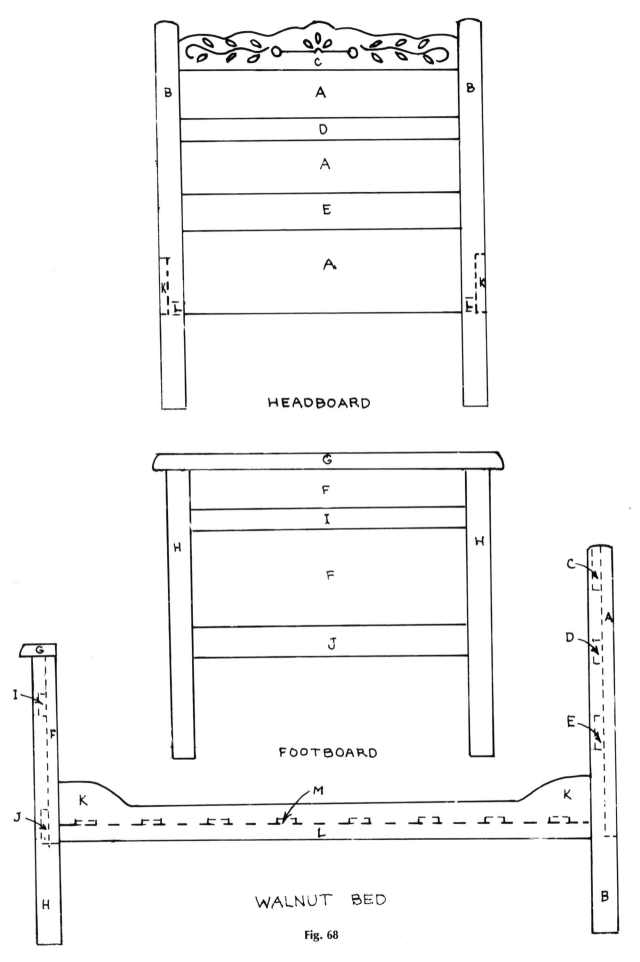

HEADBOARD

FOOTBOARD

WALNUT BED

Fig. 68

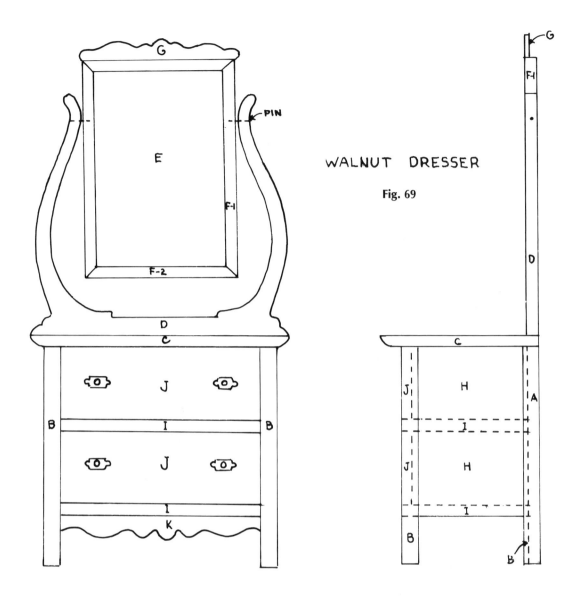

WALNUT DRESSER

Fig. 69

WALNUT DRESSER, FIG. 69

1. Prepare the following for assembly. Identify all pieces by letter.

A. Back—2 1/8″ × 1 3/4″ × 1/8″
B. Legs, cut 4—2 1/4″ × 3/16″ × 3/16″ (square)
C. Top—2 3/4″ × 1 3/4″ × 1/8″
D. Harp frame—2 3/4″ × 2 1/2″ × 1/8″
E. Mirror—2 1/4″ × 1 5/8″ tin
F-1. Mirror frame, cut 2—2 1/4″ × 1/8″ × 1/8″
F-2. Mirror frame, cut 2—1 5/8″ × 1/8″ × 1/8″
G. Mirror top—1 3/4″ × 1/4″ × 1/16″
H. Sides, cut 2—1 3/4″ × 1 1/8″ × 1/8″
I. Shelves (drawer rests), cut 2—2 1/8″ × 1 3/8″ × 1/8″
J. Drawer fronts, cut 2—2 1/8″ × 3/4″ × 1/8″
K. Apron—2 1/8″ × 1/4″ × 1/16″

2. Glue chest sides (H) between legs (B) with inside and top flush.

3. Glue chest back (A) between side units with outside back and top flush.

4. Glue shelves (I) to the inside of chest.

5. Glue top (C) to sides and back of chest.

6. Glue apron (K) between front legs and under lower shelf.

7. Glue frame to mirror (E) with mirror frames (F-1, F-2), as shown.

8. Pin mirror unit to harp frame (D).

9. Glue harp frame unit to top (C).

10. Construct drawers (J). (See Furniture Construction, Making a Drawer)

11. Attach dollhouse hardware.

BATHROOM

The wainscoted walls of the bathroom are mahogany stained, like the rest of the woodwork in the house. A claw-footed porcelain tub, pull-chain water closet, and wash basin fill this small room. A green medicine chest (see Accessories chapter) with toothbrushes, cosmetics, and medicines hangs on the wall above the basin and a towel rack is in view under the frosted high window.

FINISHED ATTIC

This room serves as a study, guest room, game room, and general hideaway. It was referred to then as the finished attic room. Today it would probably be called a family room.

The iron cot with the paisley spread wasn't very comfortable. It was Charlie's bed before he inherited the brass bed. At an early age he slept on this cot in his parent's room. (His grandfather originally had Charlie's bedroom.)

Next to the iron cot is the ever-present "spool" table, a monotonous product of the mechanized lathe.

A card table with a game of checkers awaits two players. The ladder-back chair and stool with rush seats are from an earlier time and probably relegated to the attic for that reason.

Glennie's treadle sewing machine, like most of the products of those days, was built to last. Now, nearly fifty years later, it is still being used at our summer camp (cottage). The potbellied stove with its Isinglass window was purchased not long before the "Great War" for around $20.00. Grandpa was given to making the fire hiss by spitting tobacco juice into it, but not when Glennie was looking.

The iron ice-cream parlor chair was an odd fellow put to use as a sewing machine chair. No one seems to remember where it came from.

Papers and magazines (including *Success*, which soon failed) are displayed on the old Colonial six-board chest, another piece from an earlier time. A dart board hangs on the wall above the chest and crossed swords decorate the far wall. The mirror next to the sewing machine is handy for the seamstress.

IRON COT, FIG. 70

1. Prepare the following for assembly. Identify all pieces by letter.
   A. Legs and horizontal bars, cut 8—2 1/2″ × 3/32″ × 3/32″
   B. Vertical bars, cut 6—1 1/4″ × 3/32″ × 3/32″
   C. Rails, cut 2—5″ × 3/32″ × 3/32″
   D. Braces, cut 4—3/4″ × 3/32″ × 3/32″
   E. Mattress support—5″ × 2 11/16″ × 1/32″ wood or cardboard.

2. Glue vertical bars (B) between horizontal bars (A).

3. Glue and pin headboard and footboard legs (A) to horizontal bars (A).

4. Glue and pin rails (C) to headboard and footboard one inch above floor.

5. Glue mattress support (E) to bottom of rails (C).

6. Glue braces (D) into corners at 45-degree angles.

TURTLE TOP SPOOL TABLE, FIG. 71

1. Prepare the following for assembly. Identify all pieces by letter.
   A. Top—2 5/8″ × 1 1/2″ × 1/8″
   B. Side aprons, cut 2—1 7/8″ × 3/8″ × 1/16″
   C. End aprons, cut 2— 1″ × 3/8″ × 1/16″
   D. Legs, cut 4—1 3/4″ × 3/16″ × 3/16″ (use round file)
   E. Leg base, cut 2—1 1/8″ × 3/8″ × 1/8″
   F. Shelf—1 3/4″ × 3/4″ × 1/16″

2. Glue side aprons (B) between end aprons (C) to form a rectangle that is flush at top.

3. Glue apron unit to underside of top (A).

4. Glue and pin legs (D) to bases (E).

5. Glue and pin leg units to underside of table top (A), inside apron.

6. Glue shelf (F) between legs.

7. Paint black and varnish.

CARD TABLE, FIG. 71

1. Prepare the following for assembly. Identify all pieces by letter.
   A. Top—2 1/2″ × 2 1/2″ × 1/8″
   B. Legs, cut 4—2 1/8″ × 3/32″ × 3/32″
   C. Braces, cut 4—3/4″ × 3/32″ × 3/32″

2. Glue and pin legs (B) to top (A), 3/16″ from edge of top.

3. Glue braces (C), one to each leg (B) and onto top (A).

4. Glue green felt top to table.

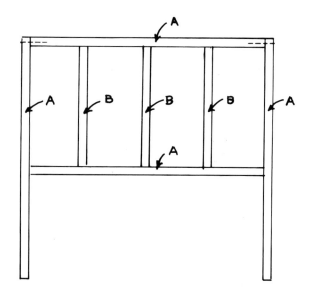

HEADBOARD AND FOOTBOARD

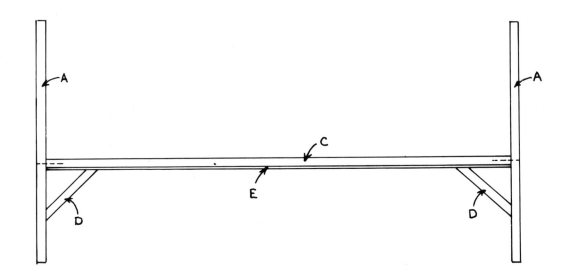

IRON COT

Fig. 70

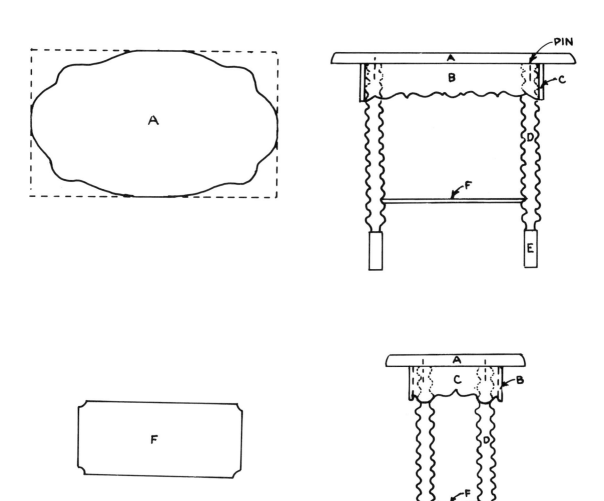

TURTLE TOP SPOOL TABLE

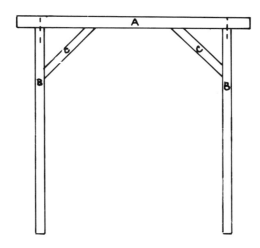

Fig. 71

CARD TABLE

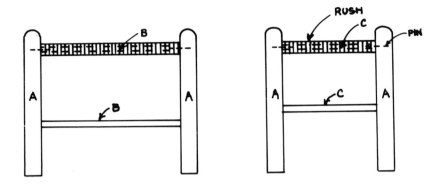

RUSH SEAT STOOL

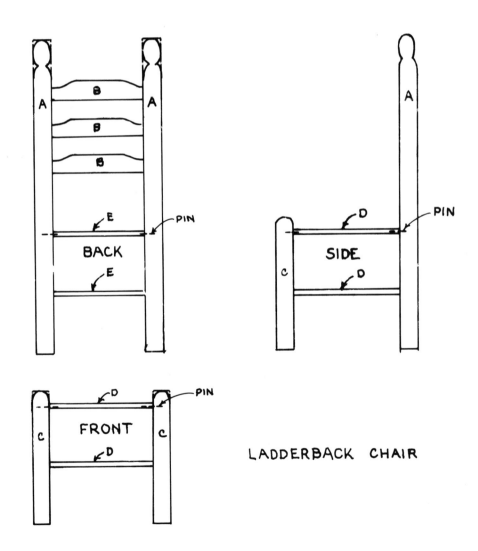

BACK

SIDE

FRONT

LADDERBACK CHAIR

Fig. 72

LADDERBACK CHAIR, FIG. 72

1. Prepare the following for assembly. Identify all pieces by letter.
   - A. Back posts, cut 2—3 1/4″ × 3/16″ dowel
   - B. Slats, cut 3—1″ × 3/16″ × 1/16″
   - C. Front posts, cut 2—1 3/8″ × 3/16″ dowel
   - D. Front and side rungs, cut 6—1 1/8″ × 1/16″ dowel
   - E. Back rungs, cut 2—1″ × 1/16″ dowel

2. Glue slats (B) between back posts (A).

3. Glue and *pin* one back seat rung (D) between back posts (A); glue the other back rung (D) between back posts (A).

4. Glue and pin front rungs (D) between front posts (C) as in step #3.

5. Glue and pin side rails (D) between front and back units, making sure that the seat rungs are all pinned.

6. Rush seat directions, Fig. 73: Cut about a yard of common kitchen string or carpet thread. Fasten the end to left hand rail (rung 1) with glue and clamp with a snap clothespin until dry. Carry cord up through center of chair seat, over and under rung 2, up through center of chair seat again, and back over itself and rung 1. Pass the cord under rung 1 and the first end of the cord. Adjust cord at corner and pull taut. The cord then goes across seat, over and under rung 3, up through center of seat, and over and under rung 2 again. Bring the cord up through center of seat and over to rung 4. Repeat this procedure until you have completed the first round, then continue the rounds until the seat is filled in. To end weaving, carry cord down through the center and tie to any cord on the bottom. If you should want to make a rush seat when the front rail is longer than the back rail, fill in the corners until a square hole is evident, beginning with rung 1 and ending with rung 3. (The ends are glued to rungs 1 and 3 as before.) Continue in the same manner as outlined above to fill in the rest of the seat.

RUSH SEAT STOOL, FIG. 72

1. Prepare the following for assembly. Identify all pieces by letter.
   - A. Legs, cut 4—1 1/2″ × 3/16″ dowel
   - B. Front and back rungs, cut 4—1 1/2″ × 1/16″ dowel
   - C. Side rungs, cut 4—1″ × 1/16″ dowel

2. Glue and pin front and back rungs (B) between legs (A), making sure the seat rung is pinned as well as glued.

3. Glue and pin side rungs (C) between legs (A), making sure again that the seat rung is pinned.

4. Rush seat as in step 6 of Ladderback Chair (Fig. 73). Stain if desired.

SIX BOARD CHEST, FIG. 74

1. Prepare the following for assembly. Identify all pieces by letter.
   - A. Front and back, cut 2—4″ × 1 1/2″ × 1/8″
   - B. Bottom—3 3/4″ × 1 3/8″ × 1/8″
   - C. Ends, cut 2—1 7/8″ × 1 3/8″ × 1/8″
   - D. Top—4 1/4″ × 1 3/4″ × 1/8″

2. Glue bottom (B) to front and back (A) where indicated on pattern.

3. Glue ends (C) between front and back (A) with tops flush.

4. Hinge top (D) with outside leather strap hinges with front extended so that it will open easily and with back flush.

5. A 1/16″ decorative wood strip may be glued above the feet, around the sides and front of the chest.

RUSH SEAT DIRECTIONS

Fig. 73

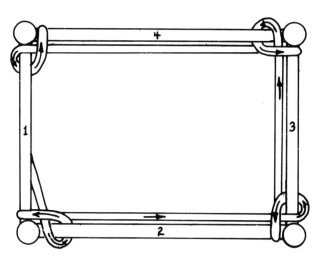

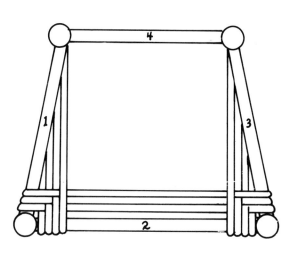

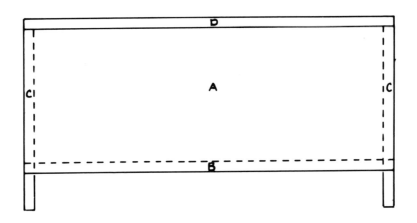

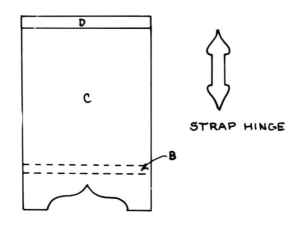

STRAP HINGE

SIX BOARD CHEST

Fig. 74

OPEN ATTIC

The open attic is used for out-of-season items as well as those no longer in use, stacked neatly around the room and in the dormer area.

The children's baby furniture, including a broken high chair and the crib on rockers, are awaiting the arrival one day of grandchildren. The two table lamps are rejects from the house (both broken, I suspect) but perhaps still usable in a pinch. Charlie's sled and wagon are temporarily stored in the attic but are available for winter snow or a hauling job that might come up. Glennie's old dress form stands neglected in the corner.

Polly's cast-off doll is sitting in the upholstered wing chair that didn't seem to fit anywhere downstairs. Old pictures and an old sampler lean against the boxes, stacked in disarray. It looks as though one of the children got into them in a hurried search for some half-forgotten treasure.

The water pitcher and wash basin, as well as the old chamber pot—no longer needed in the new house with indoor plumbing—have been gathering dust for some time.

One of my favorite pieces is the rocking horse, patiently awaiting a new master.

FOUR-POSTER BED, FIG. 75

1. Prepare the following for assembly. Identify all pieces by letter.

    A. Posts, cut 4—2″ × 3/8″ dowel

    B. Headboard—2 3/8″ × 3/8″ × 1/16″

    C. End rails, cut 2—2 1/2″ × 3/8″ × 1/8″

    D. Side rails, cut 2—5″ × 3/8″ × 1/8″

    E. Mattress rest—5 1/2″ × 3″ cardboard or wood

2. Glue one end rail (C) and headboard (B) between two posts (A).

3. Glue the other end rail (C) between the other two posts (A).

4. Glue and pin the side rails (D) between the head and foot units.

5. Glue the mattress rest (E) to the bottom of the rails, which will form a recessed area for the bedding.

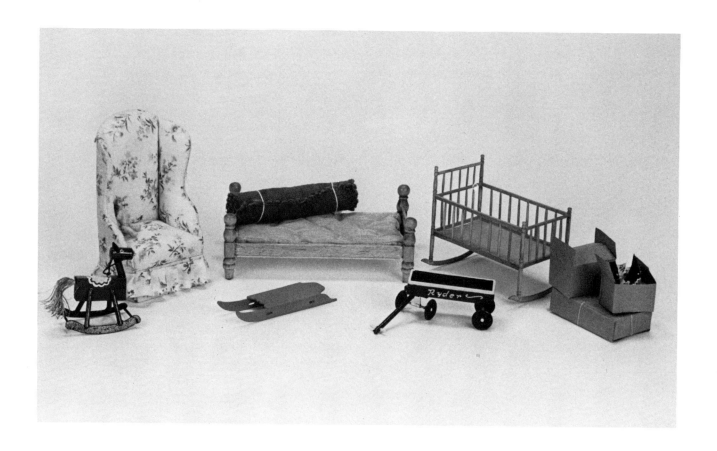

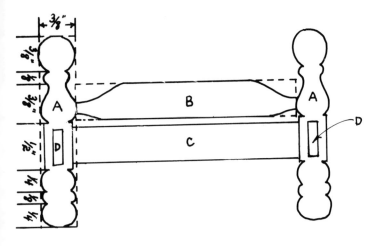

ROCKING HORSE, FIG. 76

1. Prepare the following for assembly. Identify all pieces by letter.
   A. Body—1 3/8″ × 5/8″ × 1/4″
   B. Legs, cut 4—1″ × 1/8″ dowel
   C. Rockers, cut 2—2 1/8″ × 3/8″ × 1/16″
   D. Cross bars, cut 2—1 3/16″ × 1/8″ × 1/16″
   E. Neck—1/2″ × 3/16″ dowel
   F. Head—5/8″ × 5/16″ dowel
   G. Reins—2 1/4″ carpet thread
   H. Ears, cut 2—3/16″ thin leather triangle.
   I. Tail—1 1/2″ sisal rope

2. Bevel legs (B) at angle shown and saw 1/4″ into bottoms (to insert rockers).

3. Glue legs (B) to body (A). Pin to reinforce.

4. Glue rockers (C) into slots at bottom of legs (B).

5. Glue cross bars (D) between rockers at front and back.

6. Bevel neck (E) at angle shown.

7. Saw into head (F) 1/4″ for reins.

8. Pin and glue neck (E) to head (F).

9. Pin and glue neck (E) to body (A).

10. Drill hole to insert tail (I). Paint horse basic color.

11. Glue sisal rope strands together at body end. Allow to dry. Glue into drilled hole.

12. Insert reins into mouth and tie ends.

13. Glue ears (H) in curved position to head (F).

14. Paint eyes, nose and saddle. Spray or varnish.

CARTON BOX, FIG. 76

1. Sections:
   A. Tabs for gluing
   B. Top
   C. Bottom
   D. Sides

2. Cut out box from a heavy brown paper bag around the solid lines on the pattern. Cut into tab sections between A and B.

3. Fold forward along all dotted lines starting with bottom (C).

4. Glue tabs (A) to sides (D).

5. Adjust bottom size (C) for various sized boxes.

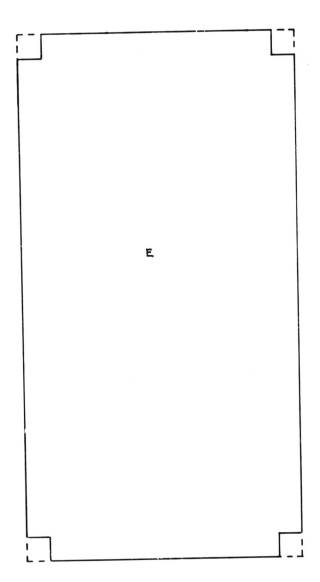

FOUR - POSTER BED

Fig. 75

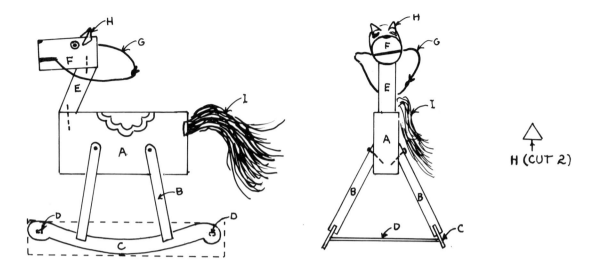

ROCKING HORSE

H (CUT 2)

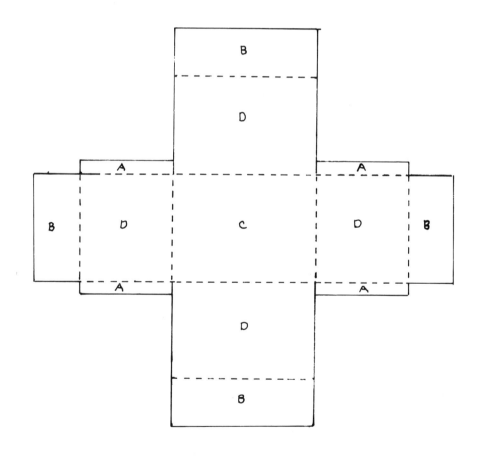

CARTON BOX

Fig. 76

CHILD'S CRIB, FIG. 77

1. Prepare the following for assembly. Identify all pieces by letter.
   A. Headboard posts, cut 2—3" × 1/8" dowel
   B. Footboard posts, cut 2—2 3/8" × 1/8" dowel
   C-1. Top horizontal bars, cut 3—1 7/8" × 3/32" dowel
   C-2. Bottom horizontal bars, cut 2—1 7/8" × 3/32" square
   D-1. Side bars, cut 2—3 1/2" × 3/32" dowel
   D-2. Side bars, cut 2—3 1/2" × 3/32" square
   E. Lower spindles, cut 30—1" × 1/16" dowel
   F. Upper spindles (headboard), cut 5—1/2" × 1/16" dowel
   G. Mattress rest—3 3/4" × 2 1/8" × 1/16"
   H. Rockers, cut 2—3" × 7/16" × 1/16"

2. Glue spindles (E, F) between horizontal bars for all four sides of crib (10 spindles for each long side of crib).

3. Saw a slot into the bottom of posts (A, B) for rockers.

4. Glue rockers (H) into slots.

5. Glue and pin spindle units to posts (A, B).

6. Cut corners from mattress rest (G) to fit on inside of posts and glue to the bottom of square horizontal bars (C-2).

SLED, FIG. 78

1. Prepare the following for assembly.
   A. Top—2 1/4" × 1" × 1/16"
   B. Runners, cut 2—3 1/2" × 1/2" × 1/16"
   C. Paint and varnish.

2. Glue top (A) to runners (B) 1/16" from side edges.

WAGON, FIG. 78

1. Prepare the following for assembly. Identify all pieces by letter.
   A. Body base—2 1/2" × 7/8" × 1/16"
   B. Sides, cut 2—2 1/2" × 5/16" × 1/16"
   C. Ends, cut 2—3/4" × 5/16" × 1/16"
   D. Handle—1 3/4" × 1/8" dowel
   E. Grip—1/2" × 1/16" dowel
   F. Tin, cut 2—1" × 1/2"
   G. Wheel base—3/4" × 1/4" × 1/8"
   H. Axle—plastic (toy)
   I. Wheels—plastic (from a toy model)
   J. Pin—sequin pin

2. Glue sides (B) and ends (C) to base (A).

3. Drill holes in handle (D) for pin (J) and grip (E).

4. Bend tin (F) around axle (H) and over at top as shown.

5. Insert wheels and axle between tin (F), pinched around axle.

6. Glue tin (F) to wheel base (G).

7. Drill hole through tin (F), wheel base (G), and body base (A) for pin. Insert pin downward through hole in base (A), through wheel base and tin. Bend up and go through handle hole. Bend point over to secure. Clip end.

8. Glue grip (E) into handle hole.

9. Glue rear wheel assembly to body (A).

10. Paint and varnish.

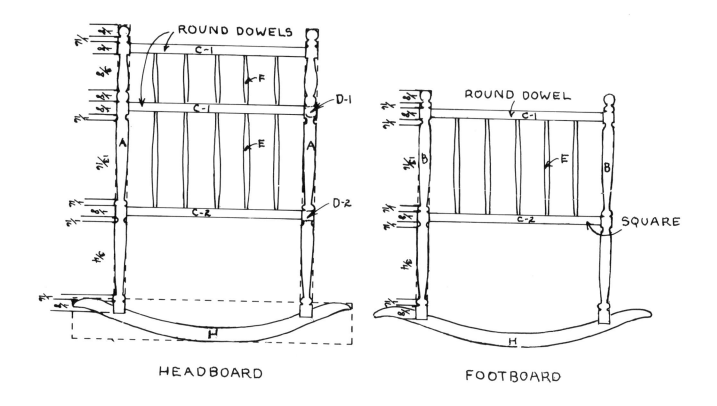

ROUND DOWELS

C-1

F

D-1

C-1

E

A   A

D-2

C-2

H

HEADBOARD

ROUND DOWEL

C-1

E

B   B

C-2

SQUARE

H

FOOTBOARD

CHILD'S CRIB

$\frac{1}{8}'' \times \frac{7}{16}''$ DOWEL CHECKERS

PAINT WHITE SQUARES RED

CHECKERBOARD

Fig. 77

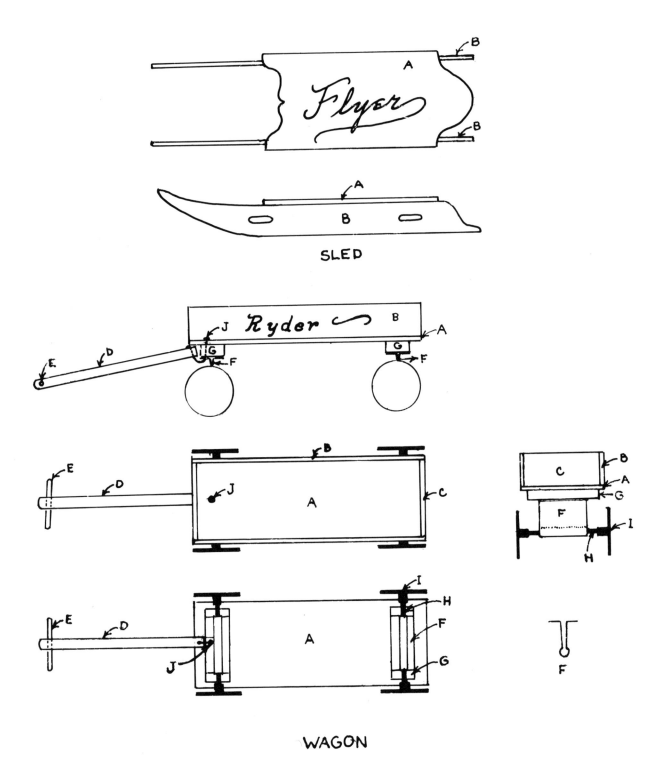

SLED

WAGON

Fig. 78

Accessories

Once your dollhouse is furnished, you will want to fill it with accessories that are typical of a 1920 home: cooking utensils, dishes, food, cleaning items, fireplace equipment, linens, books, pictures, games, and other personal effects. Accessories can be made from tin, fabric, wood, cardboard, leather, and clay as well as from jewelry findings and other "found" items.

FOUND ITEMS

To use found items, you must be creative. With your "mini-eyes" look for tiny objects that can be appropriated for dollhouse use. Hobby shops usually have an assortment of beads, chains, jewelry pins, etc. that will jog your imagination. Many of my minitreasures were found at rummage sales, flea markets, and garage sales.

There are many examples of found items in this dollhouse. The dart board in the attic was made from the face of an old compass and the crossed swords started life as plastic cocktail forks which were painted silver and black.

The table lamps, wall lights, and ceiling fixtures are all made from beads and jewelry findings. The ceiling fixture in the front hall was a lapel pin with a mustard seed enclosed in a crystall ball. It hangs from a chain-and-snap socket. The ceiling fixtures in the dining room and parlor were also lapel pins. I reshaped the "petals," added pendants and crystal beads for the "lights," and then attached the fixture to the ceiling with a sequin pin. The wall lamps in the attic and Polly's room are reshaped earrings. Of course, the brass bed (Fig. 61) is made from beads and jewelry pins as well as from wooden dowels. Toothpaste caps and cream cups (from restaurants) make excellent lampshades for the table lamps. The Handel lampshade (Fig. 92) is half of a Ping-Pong ball. The cameo in Polly's room is framed with gold filigree decoupage paper, and was once in a ring setting. The oval mirror at the foot of the steps and the Godey print in the master bedroom were also framed with gold decoupage paper.

The curtain rods are brass tubes with gold beads or sequin pins inserted and glued into the open ends. (Use contact cement (Crazy Glue) or Duco Cement for metal.) The brass rods can be purchased in hobby shops in 1/16" and 1/32" diameters. The smaller rod is inserted into the larger one for adjusting the length. The rods can be sawed to window size with the X-acto miter box and saw or a miniature hack saw. The rod holders are bent sequin pins inserted into the wooden window frames.

Curtain rods may also be made from 1/8" wooden dowels that are stained or painted gold and hung by inserting the ends into small screw eyes that can be purchased at most hardware stores.

Different sized snap assemblies—studs, sockets, and eyelets—are used for lamp parts and candlesticks.

In the dining room photos you will see a cuff link (compote), a small bell glued to a washer (covered dish), a plastic button glued to a washer (crystal flower bowl), and a toy model airplane engine (covered platter)—all are painted silver. Some of the brass articles include B-B gun shell cases and button plaques.

The sun shades on the side porch were once bamboo table mats, now painted green with cords for raising and lowering. The welcome mat at the front door was an old rubber sink stopper that came to light in a neighbor's trash.

After a long search for an appropriate floor covering for the parlor, my good friend, Mary Hinckley, came up with a piece of gift-wrapping paper that was perfect. I glued it with rubber cement to a fringed piece of unbleached muslin, ironed it, and then sprayed it with a clear acrylic spray. (Also see Floor Coverings.)

My son, Tom, who is sixteen, showed me how to use a bolt and nut to raise and lower the piano stool. Jody, my twenty-two-year-old daughter, an old hand at macrame, copied the string portieres from the 1928 Sears Roebuck catalog, a handy reference for period pieces.

The pictures and samplers are cutouts from a sales catalog, covered with acetate and framed with little pieces of wood. (Never throw your wood scraps away as they are useful for smaller items.)

An old barrel-stave trunk, made by Shackman (Japan), was doctored up for the attic. After antiquing it, the gold ribbon handles were replaced with leather ones and fastened with sequin pins (studs). The high chair in the attic is also a Shackman piece. Many times, inexpensive commercial dollhouse items can be repainted or revamped to become more authentic additions for your dollhouse.

The treadle sewing machine, the dress form, and the pot-bellied stove are Crysnbon products. They are made of plastic and come in kits which you put together. I found them easy to assemble and quite authentic in-scale reproductions. These items, along with the bathroom furnishings, would have been very difficult for the do-it-yourself enthusiast to recreate.

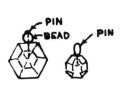

CAMEO

UMBRELLA STAND (LIPSTICK)

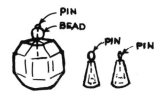

COOKIE JAR   SALT AND PEPPER

FLAT BEADS

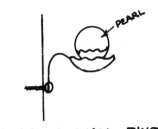

EARRING WALL FIXTURE

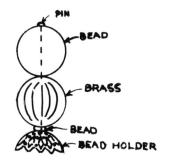

GLASS BEAD BOTTLES

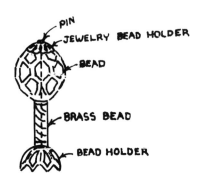

LAMPS

Fig. 79

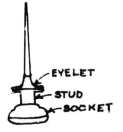

CANDLESTICKS

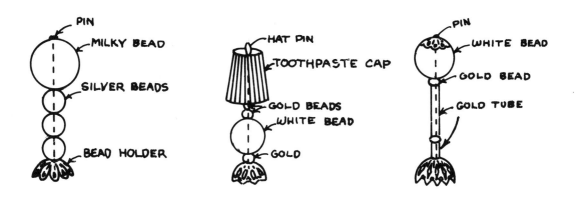

PIN
MILKY BEAD
SILVER BEADS
BEAD HOLDER

HAT PIN
TOOTHPASTE CAP
GOLD BEADS
WHITE BEAD
GOLD

PIN
WHITE BEAD
GOLD BEAD
GOLD TUBE

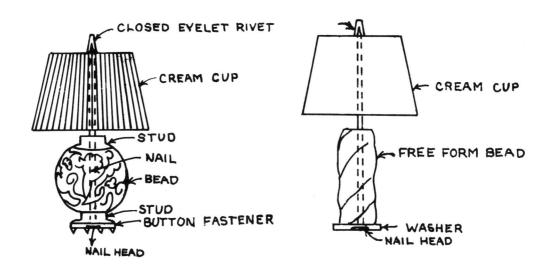

CLOSED EYELET RIVET
CREAM CUP
STUD
NAIL
BEAD
STUD
BUTTON FASTENER
NAIL HEAD

CREAM CUP
FREE FORM BEAD
WASHER
NAIL HEAD

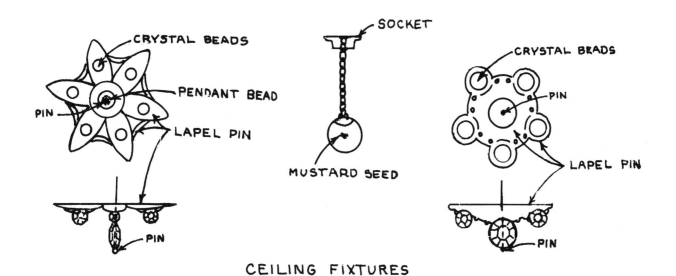

CRYSTAL BEADS
PENDANT BEAD
PIN
LAPEL PIN
PIN

SOCKET
MUSTARD SEED

CRYSTAL BEADS
PIN
LAPEL PIN
PIN

CEILING FIXTURES

Fig. 80

129

METAL AND WIRE

Metal items can be made from wire, tin cans, T.V. dinner trays, and aluminum foil, or you can buy sheets of metal at hobby shops. Some tin cans have a copper or brassy colored lining and some have a pewter-like finish on the inside. Wrought iron can be simulated by painting the tin, wire, or clay a flat black. A drop of liquid soap added to the acrylic paint will aid its adherence to metal. You will need the following materials to make metal items:

Lightweight tin cans (evaporated milk cans are good)
Wire (florist wire or wire from hobby shops which comes in different thicknesses)
Wire cutting pliers
Flat-nosed, smooth-jaw pliers (for bending and crimping)
Tin cutter (pedicure scissors work well for small pieces)
Awl or sharp pointed instrument
Tweezers
Duco cement (for china, glass, wood, metal, leather, and paper)
Contact cement (a little tricky to use but effective)

ICE CREAM PARLOR CHAIR, RUG BEATER, FLY SWATTER, AND ICE TONGS, FIG. 81

1. The chair and rug beater are made with 20-gauge wire. The seat for the chair is a 1 1/8" circle of tin. The top and legs are twisted separately and then glued under the seat. An ice cream parlor table could be made by using the chair leg pattern and increasing the size of the seat to table size.

2. The ice tongs are made either from 20-gauge wire or cut from tin.

3. The fly swatter is twisted from florist wire with a piece of tea bag mesh glued to the frame.

4. Paint all metal items black, if preferred.

SHOVEL, FUNNEL, AND BREAD KNIFE, FIG. 81

1. These items are made from tin. Bend the shovel at the dotted line and curve the forward part of the shovel until the notched edges meet. Insert the point into a wooden 1/8"-dowel handle.

2. Curve the funnel until the straight edges meet. Glue together. A nozzle may be added to the small end by gluing a rolled piece of aluminum foil to the opening.

3. The pointed end of the bread knife is glued into a wooden handle.

WOOD AND CARDBOARD

The smaller wood accessories—frames, flower pots, brooms, etc.—are made from bass, pine, or balsa wood and pine dowels. Round items can sometimes be made from lightweight cardboard, such as from a cereal or bun box. Cardboard can be bent into a desired shape more easily if it is first dipped quickly into warm water, then allowed to dry in the desired shape. Cardboard can be stained or painted to look very much like wood. Round-sided items can also be made by bending wood (See Furniture Construction, Bending Wood)

You will need the same tools and techniques for making wood and cardboard accessories as for making the furniture. (See Furniture Construction, Tools and Basic Techniques)

WALL TELEPHONE, FIG. 82

1. Prepare the following for assembly. Identify all pieces by letter.
    A. Back—2" × 3/4" × 1/16"
    B. Front—1 5/8" × 5/8" × 1/4"
    C. Shelf—3/4" × 5/16" × 1/16"
    D. Paper stop—3/4" × 1/16" × 1/32"
    E. Shelf brace—3/8" × 1/16" tin
    F. Mouthpiece base—3/16" × 1/8" × 1/8"
    G. Adjustment piece—1/4" × 1/8" tin
    H. Mouthpiece sound base—1/4"-diameter dowel, 3/32" long.
    I. Mouthpiece—11/16" × 1/4" tin
    J. Crank wire—3/8" florist wire
    K. Crank handle—1/8" toothpick dowel
    L. Receiver—3/16"-diameter dowel, 7/16" long
    M. Receiver cord—2 3/4" black carpet thread
    N. Receiver holder, cut 2—1/2" wire
    O. Bells—3/16" clay ball, cut in half

2. Glue front (B) to back (A).

3. Glue paper stop (D) to shelf (C).

4. Glue shelf (C) to front (B), as shown.

5. Glue shelf brace (E) to shelf (C) and front (B).

6. Cut 1/8" slit into center of mouthpiece base (F) for large end of tin adjustment piece (G).

7. Cut tiny slit into center of mouthpiece sound base (H) for pointed end of tin adjustment piece (G).

8. Cut and curve mouthpiece (I) into circle. (Use a tapered pencil point to curve tin.) Glue seam. Glue mouthpiece to sound base (H).

9. Glue ends of tin adjustment piece (G) and insert into mouthpiece base (F) and mouthpiece sound base (H).

10. Glue mouthpiece base (F) to front (B), as shown.

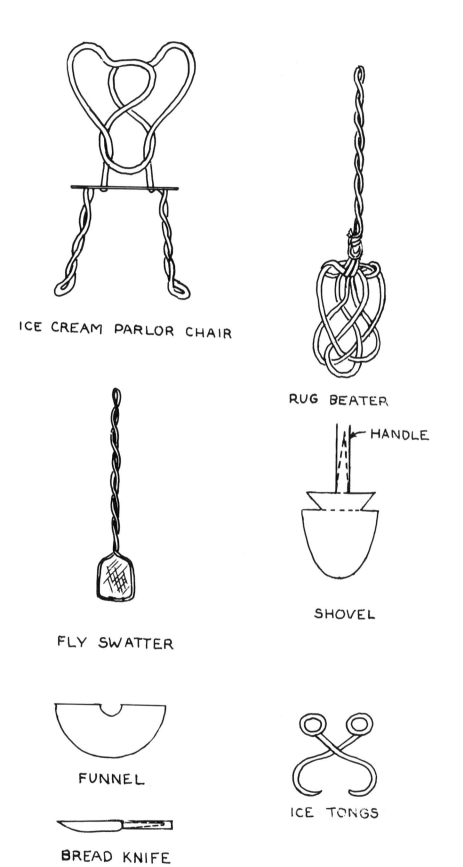

ICE CREAM PARLOR CHAIR

RUG BEATER

HANDLE

SHOVEL

FLY SWATTER

FUNNEL

BREAD KNIFE

ICE TONGS

Fig. 81

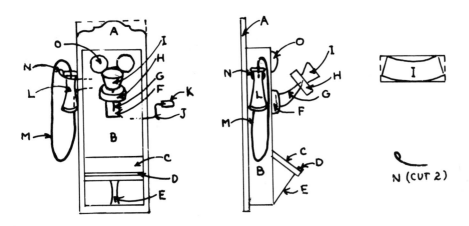

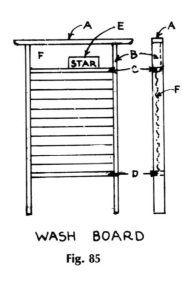

N (CUT 2)

WALL TELEPHONE

Fig. 82

WASH BOARD

Fig. 85

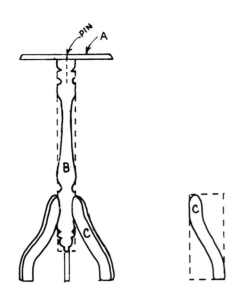

FLOWER STAND

Fig. 83

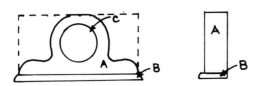

MANTLE CLOCK

Fig. 84

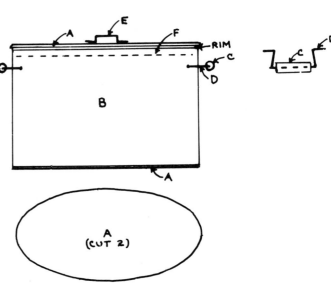

A
(CUT 2)

COPPER WASH BOILER

Fig. 86

11. Bend crank wire (J).

12. Drill hole in end of crank handle (K) and glue crank wire (J) into hole.

13. Drill hole into side of front (B) and insert crank wire.

14. Drill holes in small end of receiver (L) and into side of front (B) for receiver cord (M).

15. Glue ends of receiver cord (M) and insert into holes.

16. Drill holes for receiver holder (N) and glue wires into holes to hang receiver, as shown.

17. Paint bells (O) and glue to front (B). (Use Testers silver paint.)

FLOWER STAND, FIG. 83
1. Prepare the following for assembly. Identify all pieces by letter.
  A. Top—1″ diameter × 1/16″
  B. Post—2″ × 3/16″ dowel
  C. Legs, cut 3—7/8″ × 3/8″ × 1/16″

2. Score top around edge for a pie-crust effect.

3. Glue and pin top (A) to post (B).

4. Glue legs (C) at equal distances around post (B).

MANTLE CLOCK, FIG. 84
1. Prepare the following for assembly. Identify all pieces by letter.
  A. Body—1 1/4″ × 5/8″ × 1/4″
  B. Base—1 3/8″ × 5/16″ × 1/16″
  C. Face—7/16″ diameter cutout from a sales catalog

2. Glue body (A) to base (B).

3. Stain mahogany.

4. Glue face (C) to body (A).

5. Varnish or spray.

WASHBOARD, FIG. 85
1. Prepare the following for assembly. Identify all pieces by letter.
  A. Top—1 1/4″ × 1/8″ × 1/16″
  B. Sides, cut 2—1 3/4″ × 1/8″ × 1/16″
  C. Middle board—7/8″ × 1/16″ × 1/16″
  D. Bottom board—7/8″ × 1/8″ × 1/16″
  E. Soap—5/16″ × 1/8″ × 1/16″
  F. Copper board—1 3/4″ × 7/8″ copper

2. Bend copper board (F) with smooth-nosed pliers starting 1/4″ from end. (It must fit between C and D.)

3. Glue sides (B) to copper board (F).

4. Glue top (A), middle board (C), and bottom board (D) to copper base (F).

5. Glue soap (E) to soap rest. (I scored "STAR" into the soap bar as this was a popular brand during the 1920s.)

COPPER WASH BOILER, FIG. 86
1. Prepare the following for assembly. Identify all pieces by letter.
  A. Top and bottom, cut 2—2″ × 1″ oval (copper sheet)
  B. Sides—4 7/8″ × 1 3/8″ copper strip
  C. Side handles, cut 2—3/8″ × 3/32″ wood dowel
  D. Wire handles, cut 2—1 1/8″ florist wire
  E. Top handle—3/4″ × 1/8″ copper strip
  F. Inside lid lip—4 1/2″ × 1/8″ copper strip

2. Turn over 1/32″ (smallest amount possible) on one edge of sides (B) for top rim.

3. Bend sides (B) to fit top and bottom ovals (A). Ends should overlap slightly at one of the long sides, *not* at end curves.

4. Cut 1/16″ slits into lower edge of sides (B), around curves only.

5. Turn under 1/16″ at lower edge to form a 45-degree-angle ledge to glue the bottom to.

6. Glue ends of sides (B) together, loosening one end of rim and pressing over the other end to help hold opening together.

7. Glue bottom (A) to turned under ledge.

8. Drill hole through side handles (C), end to end.

9. Insert wire handles (D) into holes and bend wire over once to hold in place.

10. Drill holes at ends of boiler for handles. Insert wire handles (D) into holes, bend ends inside boiler to secure.

11. Bend top handle (E) and glue to center of top (A).

12. Glue inside lid lip (on edge) to bottom side of top (A).

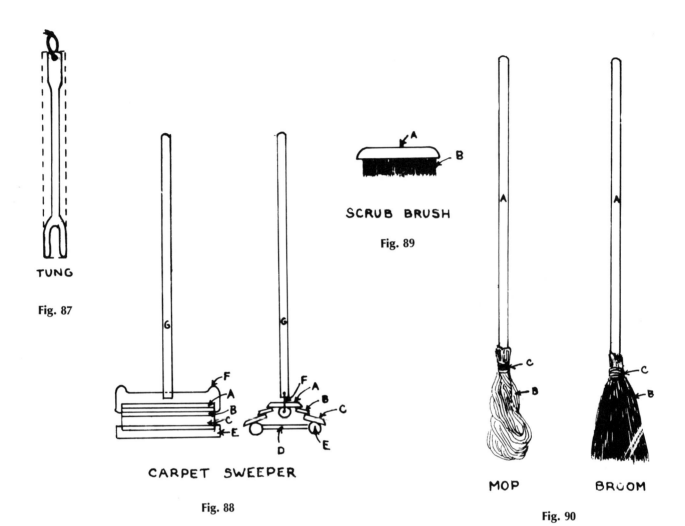

TUNG

Fig. 87

CARPET SWEEPER

Fig. 88

SCRUB BRUSH

Fig. 89

MOP   BROOM

Fig. 90

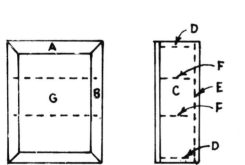

MEDICINE CHEST

Fig. 91

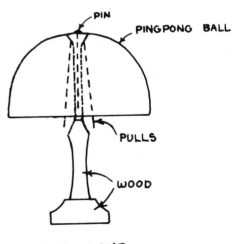

HANDEL LAMP

Fig. 92

TUNG, FIG. 87
1. Cut the tung 2 1/8" × 1/4" × 1/8".

2. Drill hole in top of stirring fork (tung) and attach a small piece of carpet thread to hang on the wall.

CARPET SWEEPER, FIG. 88
1. Prepare the following for assembly. Identify all pieces by letter.
   A. Top—1" × 3/8" × 1/16"
   B. Middle, cut 2—1" × 1/8" × 1/16"
   C. Bottom, cut 2—1" × 1/4" × 1/16"
   D. Brace—1/2" × 1/8" × 1/16"
   E. Rollers, cut 3—1 1/8" × 1/8" dowel
   F. Wire—2" florist wire
   G. Handle—3/4" × 3/32" dowel

2. Glue brace (D) between rollers (E).

3. Drill holes in both ends of third roller (E) to accommodate wire.

4. Glue roller (E) under top board (A).

5. Glue middle boards (B) to top board (A) at slight angle.

6. Glue bottom boards (C) to middle boards (B) and then to the lower rollers (E).

7. Drill hole in handle (G) to insert wire through.

8. Bend wire (F) with pliers and secure ends of wire into holes of upper roller.

SCRUB BRUSH, FIG. 89
1. Prepare the following for assembly.
   A. Top—7/8" × 1/4" × 1/8"
   B. Bristles—1/4" lengths of sisal rope

2. Shape top and glue bristles (B) to underside. Use tweezers to place bristles on top.

MOP AND BROOM, FIG. 90
1. Prepare the following for assembly.
   A. Handle—3 1/2" × 3/32" dowel
   B. Mop—3" strands of string
      Bristles—1 1/4" lengths of sisal rope
   C. Wire—fine wire or mop string

2. Fasten mop strings or bristles for broom by wrapping tightly with string or wire.

MEDICINE CHEST, FIG. 91
1. Prepare the following for assembly. Identify all pieces by letter.
   A. Door frame, cut 2—1" × 1/8" × 1/16"
   B. Door frame, cut 2—1 1/4" × 1/8" × 1/16"
   C. Sides, cut 2—1 1/4" × 7/16" × 1/16"
   D. Top and bottom, cut 2—7/8" × 3/8" × 1/16"
   E. Back—1 1/4" × 1" × 1/16"
   F. Shelves, cut 2—7/8" × 3/8" acetate
   G. Mirror—1 1/4" × 1" tin

2. Glue door frames (A, B) to mirror (G).

3. Glue top and bottom (D) to back (E).

4. Glue sides (C) to back, top, and bottom.

5. Glue shelves (F) inside chest.

6. Hinge door with paper hinges. (See Furniture Construction, Hinges)

HANDEL LAMP, FIG. 92
1. Shape wood base as shown.

2. Cut a Ping-Pong ball in half and paint a pastoral scene on the outside with water colors. Spray over paint with clear acrylic or varnish.

3. Pin shade to base top.

4. Glue carpet thread pulls in place.

5. Paint base black and varnish.

CHAMBER POT   PITCHER + BOWL

UMBRELLA

CANES

LADEL

JUGS   MORTAR AND PESTLE   FRUIT   SLICED BREAD

IRONSTONE CHINA

Fig. 93

136

CLAY

There are many commercial clays that are excellent for sculping tiny items like dishes, food, dolls, etc. (See Fig. 93.) Pendo, an air-dry clay, and Sculpy, an oven-dry clay, both work very well. The clay is fashioned into the desired shape with fingers and various tools, ranging from rolling pins to cuticle orange sticks. Small articles with sides, such as cup shapes, vases, and crocks, usually start in ball form and are then opened by inserting an orange stick or pencil into the center, forcing the clay outward. If the article has a top (jug or chamber pot), it is not necessary to have an opening, although an opening can be made *after* the clay is dry by scooping the clay out with a sharp instrument. A rolling ·pin is useful to flatten the clay before cutting lids, dishes, trays, and other flatter objects. Handles and other long, rounded forms are simply rolled with the fingers over a smooth surface. When adding bits of clay for handles and knobs, always try to blend in the clay smoothly to the main shape. Small parts may be dried separately and then glued to the main shape before being painted. The baby doll sitting in the wing chair in the attic and the loaf of bread are shaped from solid pieces of clay. The doll has separate arms and legs connected with wire. The bread is sliced *after* drying. The fruit, iced cake, and umbrella are similarly shaped from solid pieces of clay.

Clay accessories can be sanded and smoothed after drying. They can then be painted with acrylic craft paint, gold or silver, tempra, marker pens, or oil paints. A little brown may be added to soften or tone down a too-bright color. Clay articles may be sprayed with an acrylic spray, varnished, or glazed with colorless fingernail polish.

Salt dough, also called baker's dough, and bread dough can be used to make miniature food items and other accessories. Salt dough, baked brown in a bottle cap (fluted edge), makes a very realistic pie. You can also fashion your own tins for baking. Bread dough is air-dried, as are most commercial clays. Candles can be fashioned from any of these malleable materials or made from the ends of round toothpicks.

To make salt dough, combine 1 cup flour, 1/2 cup salt, and 1/2 cup water (or coffee for a light brown color). Knead the mixture and let it sit in the refrigerator overnight. Bake at 325 degrees for about 40 minutes.

Bread dough is made from 3 slices of stale white bread (remove crusts), 3 tablespoons of white glue, and 3 drops of glycerine (from your pharmacy). Tear bread into small pieces, add glue, and·mix with fingers. Knead until smooth. Water-soluble paint can be mixed with the dough until it is the desired color or dough can be painted after it is dry. Store the dough in the refrigerator until you are ready to mold it.

FABRIC

The beds all have sheets, pillows with cases, and tufted mattresses. I used a fine white cotton for the bed linens and polyester fill for stuffing the mattresses and pillows. The mattress coverings are made out of a black-and-white pin-stripe cotton. The bed linens, pillows, and curtains were machine-stitched but you may prefer to stitch them by hand. Use a small stitch setting if using a sewing machine.

One problem with sewing miniature items is that a regular double-turned hem can be too bulky. It is advisable to use a single turned-up hem. The hem can be glued, instead of sewed, but the glue will stiffen the fabric so that pleats and folds must dry exactly the way you wish them to hang.

A better solution is to pin the pleats and folds (the way they are to hang) to a piece of corrugated cardboard. Pin heads up. Spray the fabric several times with a "hard-to-hold" hair spray, allowing the fabric to dry between sprayings. When you remove the pins, the pleats and the folds will stay in place.

Towels, blankets, bedspreads, and doilies are small pieces of fabric, sometimes fringed to avoid bulky hems, or pieces of lace (cut from a larger piece) that look like crochet work. The paisley spread on the cot in the attic is a square taken from a quilt-designed fabric. Handkerchiefs are used for the curtains in Polly's room and Charlie's room.

UPHOLSTERED BEDROOM CHAIR AND FOOTSTOOL, FIG. 94

1. Cut the following from cardboard:
   A. Back
   B. Wings
   C. Seat
   D. Seat front
   E. Bottom

2. Make lightweight cardboard patterns of the back (A) including wings (B) and the seat (C & D). Shirt cardboard or typing-paper inserts are good.

3. Place the pattern of the back (A) on the wrong side of fabric and trace around the edges. Cut two back pieces.

4. Cut the fabric 1/2" from the pattern line drawn on the fabric.

5. Sew directly on the line marked on the fabric, starting at one side of the bottom and sewing around the back (and wings) to the other side of bottom. There should be an opening across the bottom.

6. Trim seam to 1/4" and clip into the edge to the stitching line around curves. Be careful not to cut stitching. Do not trim bottom.

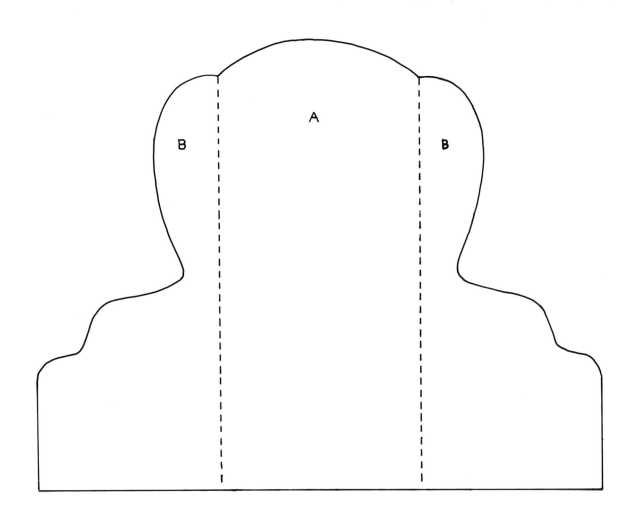

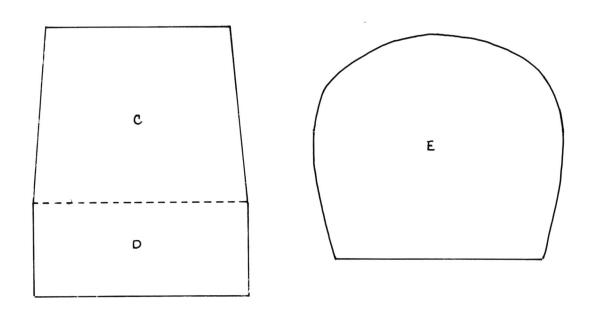

UPHOLSTERED BEDROOM CHAIR

Fig. 94

7. Turn right side out and slip cardboard pattern into the bottom opening. Keep the seam allowance on one side of the cardboard.

8. Stitch on dotted lines (shown on the pattern), starting from the top of the chair *through* the cardboard and the fabric.

9. Stuff polyester fill from the bottom into the pockets on the side of the cardboard that has the seam allowance. This side is stuffed so that the outside of the chair will be smooth. Stuff firmly around the tops with very little stuffing at the bottom. Encourage the cardboard to curve into a rounded back. Not much stuffing will go into the upper wings.

10. Sew across the bottom at the cardboard edge and then turn up and stitch the seam allowance to the inside (stuffed side).

11. Place the seat pattern (C) on wrong side of a single piece of fabric and trace around the edge.

12. Cut 1/2″ from the pattern line drawn on the fabric.

13. Place a small amount of the polyester fill between the cardboard and the wrong side of the fabric with not much fill at the front section.

14. Fold the edges of the fabric around the pattern and sew back and forth across the bottom to secure.

15. Place small end of the seat against the stuffed side of the back. Sew to the back from the underside of the chair seat. Bend at the dotted line (D).

16. Sew the front of the chair sides to the side edges of the seat.

17. Turn upside down and glue around the edges of the seat. Allow to dry in this position.

18. Cut the bottom piece (E) out of wood or heavy cardboard and glue to the bottom.

19. Cut fabric 24″ × 1″ for the flounce. Turn under and press 1/4″ hem on both long sides. Ruffle or pleat one edge.

20. Glue the ruffle to the bottom of chair. Narrow rickrack may be glued over the upper hem stitching.

21. The footstool is a covered jewelry box. Use a small amount of polyester fill for the top. Glue fabric over it and then make a ruffle as before. Glue ruffle around the side of the box.

FLOOR COVERINGS

The area rugs and stair treads used in the dollhouse came from fabric sample books. Ask your local upholstery shop for their old books. As mentioned earlier, fabrics can also be used for wallpaper.

Braided rugs are acceptable and popular in almost any period of doll house, except possibly the most elegant and luxurious of reproductions. Housewives over the years from colonial to modern times have utilized their used or leftover fabric remnants to make rag or braided rugs. Miniature-sized rugs are made exactly like their full-sized counterparts. Choose three colors of lightweight yarn and cut strands about 2 feet long but not exactly the same length. (When it is necessary to tie on more yarn to make the braid longer, the knots should not come at the same place on the braid.) Tie three even ends together and secure the knot in a drawer or under a weight so that the yarn will be taut. Make a flat braid, moving the working area farther into the drawer as you progress so that the braid will not twist. Tie on additional pieces of yarn as necessary until the braid is long enough to make a rug the desired size. Sew the braid with compatible colored thread into circular or oblong shapes, keeping the braid as flat as possible. To finish the rug, sew the end neatly together and against the last round of braid. This is called a continuous braid rug.

The braids may be different colors and patterns. Solid-color braids may be used as well as mixed-color braids. It is usually desirable to "butt" and sew the ends of a solid color braid after every round for clear definition of color. The center is a continuous braid as described above with the end secured before the butted rounds are added. Start with a lighter color in the center to avoid a bull's-eye effect and work outward, alternating dark and light shades of braid. The final round should be dark.

If you prefer a square or oblong rug with square corners, simply sew straight lengths of braid together side by side, allowing the loose ends to form fringe. Sew across both ends just before the fringe to secure.

If your rugs do not want to lie flat, iron them with a steam iron. If that doesn't work, they may be glued with rubber cement to a piece of thin paper or fabric. Weight it down with a book (between wax paper) until the glue dries. Trim the edges of the paper or fabric to the shape of the rug. If the paper shows, paint the edges to match the rug. If sewing the rug seems too difficult, the braided length of yarn may be glued directly onto a base of paper into the desired shape.

For a finer braided rug, use embroidery floss. Shape and sew as described above.

Needlepoint table top doilies make excellent rugs. Hand-woven scarfs and printed fabrics often are appropriate floor coverings. A plastic coated book jacket became the linoleum in this 1920s kitchen. Plastic-covered wallpaper sometimes can be utilized for floorcoverings and countertops. Old wallpaper sample books can often be had for the asking.

BOOK DIRECTIONS

There are various ways to construct miniature books for your dollhouse. I used an easy method which turned out to be satisfactory but there is a more sophisticated process, more like actual bookbinding, that you may wish to try.

The simplest method is to cut a piece of thin leather or cardboard for the outside cover the overall dimensions of front and back plus a bit more for the spine. Make it any size you wish, keeping in mind the scale of one inch to the foot. If you are using cardboard, you should score two "spine" lines in the center of the cardboard (wrong side) for easier bending.

Cut the pages for the book, a little smaller than the outside cover, from thin tissue paper. You will probably need five to fifteen pages, depending upon the size book you want to make. Sew along the center of the pages down the middle through all thicknesses. Use a single thread and then glue the knot and thread along the stitching line (in the back) so the thread will not come out. (See Fig. 95B)

Fold the pages in half along the stitching line. Make the fold as sharp as possible. Trim the edges evenly (the inside pages will extend out farther than the outside pages). Glue the *first* and *last* pages to the wrong side of the leather or cardboard, centered along the spine and in a *closed* position. (Glue the front page and press in place, then glue the back page and *close* the cover onto it.)

Decorate the cover and spine with acrylic paint and print the title with a very small brush. I painted the edges of the Bible pages to simulate gilting (or staining) and decorated the cover with gold paint to simulate stamping.

If you want to make a more authentic book, you can cover cardboard (the thickness of cardboard that backs a pad of paper) with thin leather, velvet, or other fabric. Cut two pieces of cardboard the exact size you want the front and back covers to be. Cut a cover for the book a little larger than the cardboard plus a bit more for the spine. Glue the front and back covers to the cover material, allowing space between the cover boards for the spine, and an equal amount around all edges. Trim the corners of the cover material to the corner points of the cardboard. (See Fig. 95A)

Prepare the pages as above. Trim the pages so that they will be a little smaller than the cover. You can simulate printed end papers by using a small patterned print for the outside pages. Use bookbinder's paper, wallpaper, or the inside of an envelope with the printed side facing each other when folded. (See Figs. 95B and C)

Fold and glue the edges of the cover material to the inside over the cardboard. Glue the first and last pages of the book to the center between the cardboard. Rub with a soft cloth to get all the bubbles out.

Decorate the cover and, if you are *really* inspired, write your own book on the blank pages.

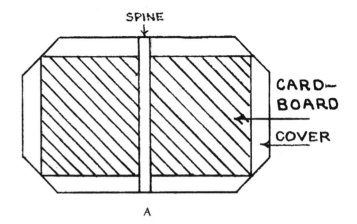

A

B

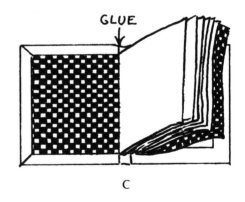

C

Fig. 95

Suppliers

AIR FERN

Also known as the Neptune plant or sea sponge, this plant needs no water or sun and is excellent for dollhouse flower arrangements. Available at flower shops.

CLAY

Patricia Memocks Originals, Inc.
P.O. Box 23187
Louisville, KY 40223
Pendo, a nontoxic clay that air dries, is available in white and fadeproof colors.

Polyform Products Co., Inc.
Schiller Park, IL 60176
Sculpy clay is also sold as Polyform in adult packaging. Elasticlay, another Polyform product, is not recommended because it tends to crumble.

DOLLS

Christine Packard
Willimantic, ME 04482
Bisque head, hands, and feet with cloth bodies in one-inch-to-the-foot scale.

Yield House
Dept. 2800
P.O. Box 1000
North Conway, NH 03860

Bee Jay's
Little World
Rt. 4
Northwood, NH 03261
Realistic, bendable dolls, inexpensively priced.

ELECTRICAL SYSTEMS

Cir-Kit Concepts, Inc.
1741 11th Ave., N.E.
Rochester, MN 55901
A tape-on miniature electrical wiring system with one-inch-to-the-foot wall outlets and ceiling fixtures that eliminates soldering. The system can be installed in new or existing houses.

Mann's E-Z Strip Wiring
Stage House Village
Scotch Plains, NJ 07076
Offers a system that requires no junction boxes, drilling, or soldering, and that can be installed after the house is built.

FURNITURE KITS

Crysnbon, Inc.
P.O. Box 13
Western Springs, IL 60558
Authentic, plastic, do-it-yourself kits, reasonably priced. (Sewing machine: Model F-200)

GRASS

Train-yard grass can be purchased in hobby shops where miniature trains are sold.

Life-Like Products, Inc.
Baltimore, MD 21203

GLUE

Connoisseur Studio, Inc.
P.O. Box 7187
Louisville, KY 40207
Decoupage Super Bond Spray, an all-purpose craft spray adhesive, was used for the grass in The "Remember When" Dollhouse.

Du Pont de Nemours, E. I. and Co.
Wilmington, DE 19898
Duco Cement is excellent for china, glass, wood, metal, leather, and paper.

Devcon Corp.
59 Endicott Street
Danvers, MA 01923
Epoxy Super Glue (2-Ton) comes in two tubes that have to be mixed. It's good for practically anything if the item can be held together until set.

Woodhill Chemical Sales Corp.
P.O. Box 7183
Cleveland, OH 44128
Super Glue, one of the instant contact cements is good for small articles that can't be clamped or otherwise held together until set.

Solomon's Laboratories
Long Island, NY 101
Sobo Glue, a white, clear-drying glue, is good for wood, fabric, leather, paper, plastic foam, and glitter. Quik Glue is good for adhering plastics to porous surfaces such as acetate "glass" to the wood frames.

Bill Muller
Wooden Toys
Telford, PA 18969
Mini-Hold adhesive is reusable and will hold tiny dollhouse items in place without gluing.

HARDWARE
Miniature Mart
1807 Octavia Street
San Francisco, CA 94109

Architectural Model Supplies, Inc.
115-B Bellam Boulevard
P.O. Box 3497
San Rafael, CA 94902
AMSI distributes furniture kits, dollhouse accessories, scaled building materials, and tools.

METAL SHEETS
Hammett's School Supplies
L. J. Hammett Co.
Cambridge, MA
A great source for all sorts of craft materials.

PAINTS AND STAINS
Acrylic paints are available in most craft and hobby shops. They are permanent, water-reducible, easily mixed, and quick drying.

Testor's Corp.
620 Buckbee Street
Rockford, IL 61101
Testor's PLA silver and gold metalic paints are excellent for painting practically any surface—tin, wood, clay, etc.

Min-Wax Co., Inc.
Clifton, NJ 07014
Stains for all kinds of wood.

PINS
Scovill Sewing Notions Division
Watertown, CT 06795
Pintique Sequin Pins are available in gold or silver finish and various sizes. Most often used for miniature work is the small, no. 8 size (one-half inch long).

TOOLS
Sears Roebuck has a good line of miniature shop tools, inexpensively priced.

Hard To Find Tools
Peterboro, NH 03458

WALLPAPER
J. Hermes
P.O. Box 23
El Monte, CA 91734

Yield House
P.O. Box 1000
North Conway, NH 03860
Carries a brick paper for chimneys, fireplaces, etc.

WOOD
Northeastern Scale Models, Inc.
P.O. Box 425 N
Methuen, MA 01844
Specializes in basswood moldings.

Miniature Makers
Evansville, WI 53536
Oak, walnut, mahogany, and pine are available.

Index